THE X RESOURCE

ISSUE SEVEN

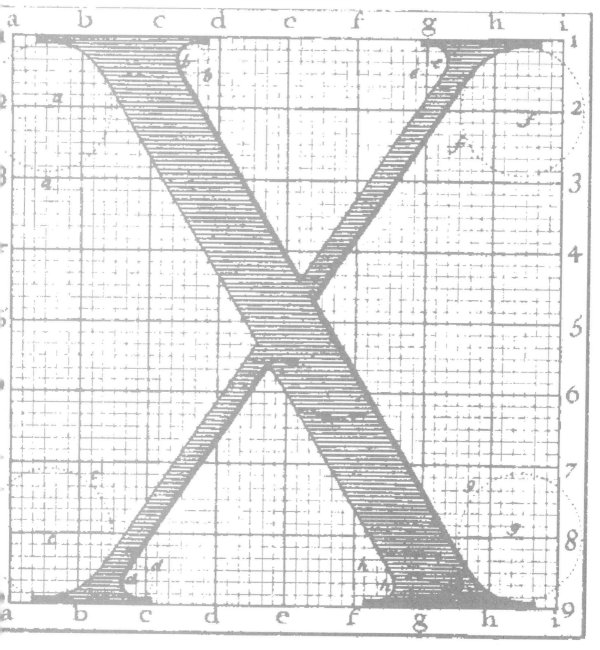

O'Reilly & Associates, Inc.

A PRACTICAL JOURNAL OF THE X WINDOW SYSTEM

THE X RESOURCE

TABLE OF CONTENTS

A PRACTICAL JOURNAL OF THE X WINDOW SYSTEM

THE X RESOURCE

TABLE OF CONTENTS, *CONTINUED*

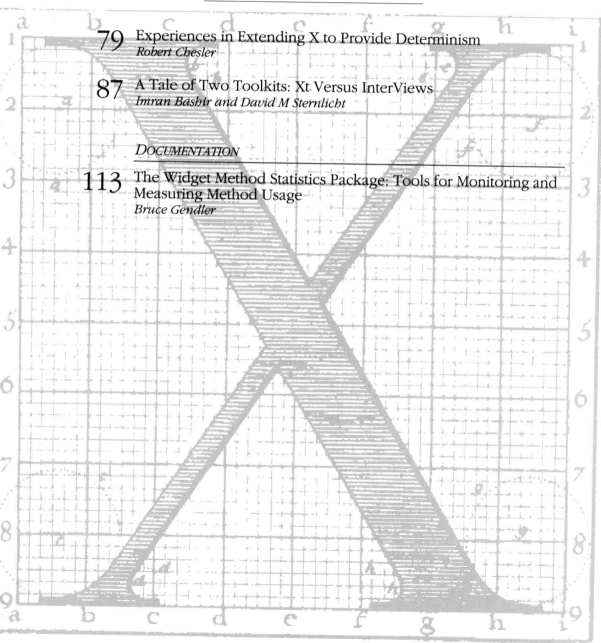

ISSUE SEVEN

THE X RESOURCE: A PRACTICAL JOURNAL OF THE X WINDOW SYSTEM

O'Reilly & Associates, Inc.

The Official Publisher of the
X Consortium's X Technical Conference Proceedings
and approved publisher of X Consortium public review specifications.

PUBLISHER

Tim O'Reilly

EDITOR

Adrian Nye
(O'Reilly and Associates, Inc.)

CONSULTANT

Alain Hénon
(Usenix Association, O'Reilly and Associates, Inc.)

EDITORIAL ADVISORY BOARD

Jeff Barr (Visix Software, Inc.)
David Bealby (Sun Microsystems)
Todd Brunhoff (Tektronix Resource Labs)
Kevin Calhoun (Informix Software)
Ellis Cohen (Open Software Foundation)
Wayne Dyksen (Dept. of Computer Science, Purdue University)
Jim Fulton (Network Computing Devices, Inc.)
Ronald Hughes (CrossWind Technologies, Inc.)
Bob Joyce (Aspect, Inc.)
Phil Karlton (Silicon Graphics, Inc.)
John Koegel (University of Lowell)
Mark Linton (Silicon Graphics, Inc.)
Chris Peterson (Integrated Computer Solutions, Inc.)
Ralph Swick (Digital Equipment Corporation)
Bob Scheifler with the staff (X Consortium) (acting as a single board member)

CUSTOMER SERVICE AND ADMINISTRATION

Cathy Record

COPY EDITING

Barbara Milligan

COVER AND INTERIOR FORMAT DESIGN

Edie Freedman

PRODUCTION

Mike Sierra

ILLUSTRATIONS

Chris Reilley

FROM THE EDITOR

First this month is a column by X Consortium Director Robert Scheifler. It provides an interesting peek into the kinds of decisions the Consortium makes at the protocol level, and at the same time points out some of the common issues involved in different past and future projects of the Consortium.

UPCOMING CHANGES AT X CONSORTIUM

As you may know, the X Consortium is separating from MIT to become a nonprofit corporation. R6, due in early 1994, will be a product of the new X Consortium. Lu Abel has been selected to be the president of the new consortium. We have included an article that explains why the X Consortium is separating from MIT and describes the selection and background of the new president.

HIGHLIGHTS OF THIS ISSUE

We start with an article on an audio interface to X developed at Georgia Tech. Recent legislation requires that employers provide access to blind and visually impaired users, so it's important to see and understand how X can comply. You may have read the paper from the same group on this topic in Issue 5, but this article is much more extensive and is valuable even to readers of the previous article. The X Consortium has agreed to adopt into the R6 version of Xt some of the features suggested by this article.

Robert Chesler has written a paper about how X can be adapted for real-time applications, based on his experience at Concurrent Computer Corporation.

George Ross of the University of Edinburgh describes his department's approach to managing a large network based on X. He has made available some of the utilities they have developed to simplify administration.

As part of an internship at the X Consortium, Imran Bashir, along with former Consortium staff member David Sternlicht, wrote a paper comparing InterViews with Xt. Since Inter-Views is the basis of Fresco, the next-generation C++ toolkit for X, it is time to begin learning about it. The paper develops the same application with both tools and describes the lessons learned about the advantages and disadvantages of each toolkit.

Yours truly has written an article about X application debugging. The intention is to bring together tips from various experienced programmers and my own experience to provide the most complete description of debugging available anywhere. If you have any suggestions for improving this article, please let me know, since we intend to use it in a future book.

Finally, the documentation section covers the Widget Method Statistics Package. This package allows you to profile widget methods on an instance-by-instance basis and thereby optimize widget operations or learn more about how the Xt Intrinsics operate.

BIBLIOGRAPHY AVAILABLE FOR FTP

Nelson H. F. Beebe of the University of Utah maintains a bibliography of all articles that have appeared in *The X Resource* since Issue 0. The files are on *ftp.math.utah.edu* in the directory *pub/tex/bib/xres.**. The files are in bibtex format. The bibliography is normally updated as soon as Nelson receives his copy. Our thanks to Nelson for providing this valuable service.

CODE EXAMPLES FOR ISSUE 6

Seven of the articles in Issue 6 have example code available in *The X Resource* code archive. However, some of those articles did not explicitly give filenames or locations, or when they did they are difficult to find. Please see the list of contents for *The X Resource* code archive on page 7 for this information.

Adrian Nye.

THE X RESOURCE CODE ARCHIVE

The following table describes the current contents of this archive, followed by where you might look for updated versions of each piece of public domain software. See Issue 3 for a complete description of how to get these files by *ftp*, ftpmail, bitftp, or *uucp*.

DESCRIPTION	FILENAME
Issue 0:	
Free Widget Foundation widgets	*fwf.shar.Z*
Cornell University widgets	*xcu.v1.6.tar.Z*
TekColor editor	*xtici.tar.Z*
(The Wcl Table widget is in the Wcl distribution under Issue 3)	
Issue 1:	
MIT conference proceedings (no files for ftp)	
Issue 2:	
Motif/C++ class library	*GINA++1.6.tar.Z*
Widget Creation Library	*Wcl-2.2.tar.Z*
Issue 3:	
MultiUser Xt Application Demo	*MultiUserVote.tar.Z*
XamineYourZerver extension	*XYZext.tar.Z*
Font Server Extensions	*hp_xlfd_enhancements/*
patches	*hp_xlfd_patches.public.tar.Z*
demo programs	*hp_xlfd_demo.tar.Z*
utility functions	*hp_xlfd_utils.tar.Z*
RichText widget	*XcRichText-1.2.tar.Z*
Issue 4:	
RPC in X application demos	*rpc.tar.Z*
xgen GUI scripting language	*xgen.tar.Z*

TABLE 1: *THE X RESOURCE CODE ARCHIVE—CURRENT CONTENTS*

DESCRIPTION	FILENAME
Finding Auxiliary Files	*XmtFindFile.tar.Z*
Cmap and Hdial widget	*cwikwidget.tar.Z*
X Input Extension	*cube.c*
Issue 6:	
Motif Subclassing	*Subclassing.tar.Z*
Interprocess Communication in Xt Programs	*ipc.tar.Z*
Context Help in Motif	*helpdemo.tar.Z*
Xhelp help system	*xhelp.tar.Z*
Font Handler Package	*Font_Hand_1.0.tar.Z*
DASH and Xj toolkit	*DASH.1.1.tar.Z*
Xhyper help system	*xhyper-1.2.tar.Z*

TABLE 1: *THE X RESOURCE CODE ARCHIVE—CURRENT CONTENTS (CONTINUED)*

Some of the software listed in Table 1 may be periodically updated, and we may not always have the latest version in our archive. You may want to look in the *contrib* directory on *export.lcs.mit.edu* to see if a later version is available there.

8TH ANNUAL X TECHNICAL CONFERENCE

"The Designers' X Conference"
Call for Papers, Talks and Tutorials

The 8th annual X Technical Conference will be held on January 24–26, 1994 at the Marriott Copley Place Hotel in Boston, Massachusetts. The conference is sponsored by the X Consortium. A thousand attendees, including experts from both industry and academia, come together for three days to discuss the very latest problems, solutions, and research. There is no set theme for the conference; we are interested in submissions covering all aspects of X. Presentations on both research and commercial developments are encouraged.

The first day of the conference will be devoted to tutorials. We are interested particularly in tutorial topics that have not been given before or that have had only limited exposure. Proposals for tutorials that might draw only a small audience are quite welcome. Tutorials are usually half day (three hours) or all day (six hours). We do not pay tutorial speakers a fee. We do cover the cost of printing tutorial notes. We can within reason provide projection equipment for computers, but you need to provide the computer.

The final two days will be devoted to talks, in a single track. Presentations can range from 5 to 50 minutes, and videotape is welcome (but live computer projection is not available). Written papers are not required; however, the conference proceedings will be published as an issue of the *The X Resource*, by arrangement with O'Reilly & Associates, Inc. The issue will be available both at and after the conference. So, this is an ideal opportunity to reach a large X community, with rapid publication.

On all three days there will be "Birds of a Feather" sessions for general discussion of areas of specific interest to the attendees. If there are particular BOFs you would like to see or run, please let us know.

No trade show or vendor exhibits will be associated with this conference.

If you would like to give a tutorial, make a presentation, or run a BOF, or if you have a different creative proposal, send details to:

xconference@expo.lcs.mit.edu

or to:

Bob Scheifler
Laboratory for Computer Science
545 Technology Square
Cambridge, MA 02139

Network mail is preferred. Please be sure to include your name, net and postal address, phone number, affiliation, a detailed description of the presentation, what your relationship is to the work (e.g., project manager, principal designer, lead engineer, me-myself-and-I), how much time you need for the presentation, and what A/V facilities you need. Generally, the more information you supply the program committee, the better. Rough drafts and outlines are encouraged.

The deadline for submissions is October 28; receipt will be acknowledged. Talk and tutorial proposals must be received by midnight, October 28, Eastern time. No exceptions. The program committee cannot consider any submissions received after this deadline.

Please be aware that the deadline for camera-ready copy of final papers for accepted talks is December 13. Notification of acceptance will happen around November 10.

The conference registration fee is waived for speakers.

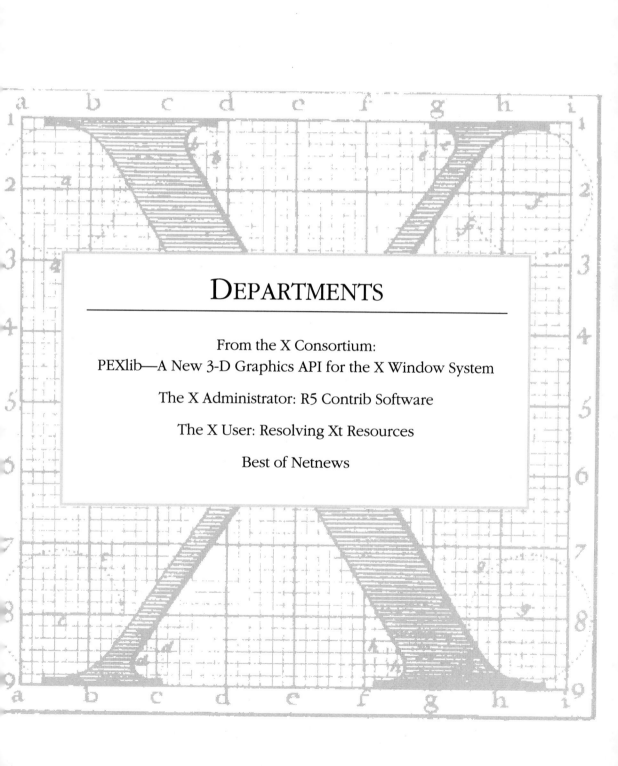

DEPARTMENTS

FROM THE X CONSORTIUM:

BUDDY, CAN YOU SPARE AN RPC?

Robert Scheifler

When should you use the X protocol? It seems like such an innocent question.

The first time I recall really banging into this question was during the public review of the *ICCCM (Inter-Client Communications Conventions Manual)*. One comment received in March 1989 started out with this sentence: "Peer-to-peer communications via an X server is an unwise precedent to set." The specific complaint was the use of the X protocol for exchanging cut-and-paste data between clients. While it might be argued that there is reasonable justification for having the X server arbitrate selection ownership, using properties on windows to exchange the actual data is surely as inappropriate as using the X server to provide general file transfer (FTP) or electronic mail (SMTP) service.

One of the arguments cited in favor of using the X protocol was cross-transport interoperability. Client A talks to the X server over TCP, client B talks to the same X server over DECnet, and the X server makes it possible for these clients to exchange data even though they cannot talk directly to each other. The obvious response is that the X server is not magic; one can build protocol conversion gateways, and doing so satisfies other demands for process-to-process communication beyond X cut and paste. X is but one component of an overall distributed system: solve a networking problem at the networking level, not at the user interface.

Another discussion point was that formal standards for process-to-process communication were under development—for example, in the IEEE POSIX committees—and that the X Consortium should leverage them. The response was that the X community could not wait for formal standards and therefore a solution was needed immediately. Indeed, today P1003.12 (Protocol Independent Interfaces) is still only in draft form, there is no standard for RPC (Remote Procedure Call), OSI (Open Systems Interconnection) protocols have not taken the world by storm, and CORBA (Common Object Request Broker Architecture) implementations are not yet widely available. Is coherent networking really one of the things that distinguishes Us from the Competition?

Robert Scheifler is Director of the MIT X Consortium.

A third concern was that if data interchange was defined as a separate (not-over-X) protocol, it would fall outside the purview of the X Consortium and we would end up with no standard at all. I fear that back then, before I had gray hairs, I too actually believed this. In retrospect, I am not quite sure why I believed it. A few months earlier we had presented a proposal within the X Consortium to standardize XDMCP (X Display Manager Control Protocol) as an independent protocol, and eight months earlier X Consortium discussions about font support had led to initial agreement that a font server was a good way to support large numbers of displays without having to replicate font data. Now, XDMCP was clearly specific to X, but with the font server protocol there was some tension. A protocol defined solely to communicate X font data to X servers was within our charter, but was it reasonable to limit the design in that way? Wouldn't it be desirable to have printers obtain font data from the same font server? How about other window systems? But if the protocol covered a broader scope, was it still reasonable for the X Consortium to define the standard? I think the same underlying concerns were present for the ICCCM: that if data exchange was divorced from the X protocol it would be clearly revealed as a mechanism with broad applicability, and that the X Consortium would not be the appropriate forum for producing such a standard.

Time-to-market considerations essentially made this particular ICCCM discussion academic, and the selection mechanism became a standard. An effort was made to not preclude the use of the font server by printers or other applications, but the design focus continued to be supplying X-oriented data to X servers.

Within a year of the selection mechanism becoming standard, interesting uses of it started to appear. One was *editres*, a resource editor that allows users to customize a running application. *editres* uses a protocol between the editor and the application to convey structural information and resource alterations. A single protocol exchange is a combination of a synthetic ClientMessage event and two X selection conversions with an exchange of selection ownership. The selection mechanism was used because it was the standard for data exchange, and the initial ClientMessage was necessary to get the exchange started because the selection mechanism worked "backward" in this case. Altogether, a single logical exchange involves about 16 independent messages and 5 complete round trips between the two clients, all routed through the X server. You might wonder if this is necessary complexity until you realize that it is a substitute for what ought to be a single remote procedure call!

Release 5 brought the concept of Input Method (IM) servers to X. Keyboard input of Asian languages can require fairly complex language engines, large dictionaries, and auxiliary user interface support, and a common implementation strategy is to encapsulate this into a separate server whose state can be shared among all of a user's applications. There are two IM server protocols implemented in R5, but neither is a standard; R5 focused on standardizing the Xlib API. To provide interoperability, however, the question of a standard protocol between applications and the IM server does arise, and the X Consortium is currently working on one. As you might guess, the question also arises as to whether this protocol should be layered on top of the X protocol or whether it should be an independent protocol.

One argument given for using the X protocol is that clients on independent subnets A and B might be able to connect to an X server on subnet C but might not be able to connect directly between subnets A and B because of security constraints or routing limitations. Therefore, if the IM server is on one of those subnets, not all clients will be able to connect to it. This is just a variation of the DECnet/TCP argument. Clearly the X server demonstrates the ability to implement a gateway between the two subnets; it demonstrates also that no real security wall exists between the two subnets.

Another argument for using the X protocol is that X-specific data (such as window IDs) is exchanged over the IM protocol, so it somehow makes more sense to transmit that data over the X protocol. The same kind of argument was raised during the discussions on drag and drop and insets (which we'll discuss in a moment). Although one response is that the data types are not relevant to the issue, in this particular case a better response is that we should look at where the data is X-specific and see if we can generalize it. The services provided by an Input Method server are equally useful in character-based (*tty*) applications (yes, they still exist), and to a certain extent might be useful in some offline processing. A single protocol covering all of these situations seems desirable.

Perhaps a more compelling argument is that using a separate protocol would break binary compatibility with R5. The current Xlib interface does not admit the existence of an IM server; Xlib exports only one file descriptor, for the connection to the X server. It is quite common for applications (or toolkits on their behalf) to block in a "select" or "poll" system call until a file descriptor is ready for processing. The file descriptor for the X server is obtained from Xlib and is merged with other file descriptors used by the application. If existing applications were relinked against a new Xlib that used a separate IM protocol, they would fail to wake up and respond to messages from the IM server, because the IM file descriptor would not be included in the select/poll set. Because binary compatibility is very important, this in a sense is a "good" argument for using the X protocol. However, it is really just a reflection that we should have considered this issue more carefully when the new Xlib IM functions were first designed. If there was a standard for RPC (the IM protocol semantics map easily into a simple RPC model), we almost certainly would have agreed long ago on a dispatch framework that allowed for the transparent, binary-compatible addition and removal of RPC-based services. At the present time, the IM protocol is being specified so that it can be used both over a direct transport and layered on the X protocol.

Another area of active development in the X Consortium is session management. The original proposal was a logical extension of the partial facilities provided in the first *ICCCM* standard; clients decorate their top-level windows with properties for the session manager to find, and various ClientMessage events are sent through the X server to cause actions, such as checkpoint and shutdown, to be performed. This seems fine until one considers that a session might well include processes that are not X clients, and that the user wants their state preserved and wants them restarted along with the X clients when the session is reactivated. There are also some problems with making the solution "recurse"; for example, when a mail handler spawns an editor to compose a message, the mail handler really needs to act as a nested session manager for the editor, rather than have the editor handled directly by the top-level session manager.

Once again, a discussion ensued about the merits of using the X protocol. Once again, the "DECnet cannot talk to TCP" argument was raised and refuted. It was argued that using a non-X protocol was "hard" while using the X protocol was "easy," even though the same set of difficult semantic questions had to be answered in either case, and the details of transport handling had already been coped with in the X server, the font server, and elsewhere. Once again it was argued that if we tried to encompass non-X applications in the definition of a session, then session management would no longer fall within the charter of the X Consortium and we would have to look to some other body to standardize it. Now older and grayer, I was willing to answer that our members say they need it and appear to believe that no one else can supply it, so I was willing to be pragmatic and make it our problem. The specification that is now nearing completion is not layered on the X protocol.

An attempt to develop a standard drag-and-drop protocol has been in progress for some time within the X Consortium. Both the drag and the drop phases require data exchange between the client initiating the drag and the client that holds the drop site. Naturally, the question of whether or not to use the X protocol has again been a topic of discussion, but with some new twists. The counterproposal was not to have the clients communicate directly with each other using a non-X protocol, but to have them communicate indirectly through a "drag server" using a non-X protocol.

The client initiating the drag has to be able to find potential drop sites and, as the object is dragged around the screen, has to determine what drop site the object is currently over. One method is to find all of the top-level windows on the screen, look for windows with properties indicating they are drop sites, and select for Enter and Leave events on those windows. There are several problems with this approach. It restricts you to drags that are initiated using the pointer, which in turn precludes simultaneous drags (for example, from autonomous agents providing visual feedback of their actions). If you try to drag a small window around the screen for visual feedback, rather than just change the X cursor shape, it is difficult to receive pointer events on the "real" windows because the feedback window is generally the one under the cursor. The mechanism breaks down in a secure environment such as a CMW (Compartmented Mode Workstation) environment, in which clients are not normally permitted to obtain any information about other clients (including the IDs of their windows) without going through a trusted intermediary. Finally, if the screen has a mixture of X windows and "foreign" windows (for example, in a Windows or Macintosh environment), there is no ready path for supporting drag and drop between X and non-X windows.

The interposition of a drag server deals with all of these problems, although I will not try to detail the reasons here. Basically, the client initiating the drag can communicate absolute screen coordinates (independent of how they are obtained) to the drag server, which calculates the correct drop-site and informs the appropriate client, and the drag server acts as an intermediary for passing data between the two clients, without revealing the identity of one client to another. The drag server does not need to use Enter and Leave events, can readily distinguish drop site windows from drag-feedback windows, and can act as a gateway for foreign windows. You might still think about communicating with the drag server over the X protocol, but that would effectively double the number of round trips and context switches per logical exchange, which is easily demonstrated to result in unacceptable performance on low-end systems. So, we are led to a design using a drag server and a non-X protocol.

Recently within the *ICCCM* working group there has been some discussion of *insets*, meaning the embedding of a window from one client inside a window of another client— for example, a spreadsheet embedded in a document editor. The initial proposal is for the clients to use X protocol mechanisms to negotiate with each other. The *ICCCM* geometry mechanisms used between top-level windows and a window manager can be recursively applied (with some changes) to control the geometry of inset windows. Window properties can be used to describe requirements for grabs, resources, and input propagation. The selection mechanism can be used to communicate requests for menu bar entries. However, one of the issues raised about the proposal is that the two clients will need to cooperate in other areas. For example, how do they communicate to produce combined output when the user selects Save, Print, or some other semantic action from the menu bar? Assuming there is a protocol for such communication, why shouldn't it be used for all of the inset-oriented communication? Do synchronization or other problems arise if the protocols are separate?

A related X Consortium activity under way is Fresco,[†] a new API for building graphical user interfaces that integrates functionality from several areas, including window systems, widget sets, structured graphics, document layout, and application embedding. Fresco is designed to use the OMG (Object Management Group) CORBA system to handle interclient messaging, including the messaging needed to support application embedding. How does Fresco's approach to embedding mesh with a proposal to use the X protocol for some of the communication? You will note that here I have questions and not answers; the discussion of inset protocols and interoperability is still at a fairly early stage within the X Consortium, and I do not know yet what is the right design.

Most of the protocols discussed here (XDMCP, font server, *editres*, IM server, session manager, and drag and drop) are very simple protocols that would map in a straightforward manner into almost any basic RPC mechanism. Well, almost. Many of the protocols depend on a notion of "connection," and attach meaning to closing the connection, including the case when the connection is closed because a client crashes. RPC mechanisms tend to provide only connectionless semantics, so this is a problem. Still, I believe that an RPC standard, appropriately designed, would have been a significant help to us over the years. Doubtless the X Consortium has not designed its last protocol standard, so buddy, can you spare an RPC?

---

† Fresco is a registered trademark of the Massachusetts Institute of Technology.

THE X CONSORTIUM:

THE NEXT GENERATION

The X Consortium is spinning out of MIT as of the end of 1993. Several causes prompt this change: a desire to be unfettered by academic salary limits in attracting and retaining a topnotch staff, an inconsistency between MIT's goals (education and basic research) and the Consortium's. But what crystalized the decision was Bob Scheifler's desire, after nearly a decade of being "Mr. X," to move on to something else.

When Bob's and MIT's desires were made known, a subcommittee of Consortium members was formed to determine its future. The Future Committe considered affiliating with an existing industry-sponsored consortium, but none could easily accomodate the Consortium's business model. The decision was therefore made to establish the Consortium as an independent not-for-profit organization. A nationwide search was started for someone with the right mix of business and technical skills to lead the new organization.

Lu Abel has been selected as the new President of the X Consortium after it's separation from MIT at the end of 1993.

FROM LUTHER C. ABEL

It's an incredible personal honor to have been the one selected.

Actually creating the new organization has been an adventure. We're forming a new company! A business plan has been drafted, and we have to deal with lawyers, accountants, landlords, network connections, and a million other details. But this new company is also an unusual one—it's one with an established product and market. More important, it has an established way of doing business, an established ethos. The new Consortium must reflect all this. And we must plan and do everything possible to effect a smooth transition out of MIT.

So where are we and where are we going? The new X Consortium (NXC, for short) has been incorporated. A business plan and By-laws for NXC have been presented to members of the MIT X Consortium. By the time you read this, we will have selected a physical location and signed a lease.

We expect to move people, both physically and as employees, out of MIT and into the new consortium over the summer. Happily for all of us, most of the existing MIT staff will join NXC. Moving MIT computer resources to NXC will be a delicate task, expecially since we will be in the middle of finalizing R6 alpha!

Although R6 was originally expected to be MIT's swan song, as we more clearly see both the R6 schedule and the required schedule for moving away from MIT, R6 will definitely be a product of the new Consortium. It will be a challenge to make a smooth transition and keep R6 on schedule, but I am also looking forward to establishing NXC's credibility as MIT's successor by delivering a quality product on schedule.

I look forward to sharing more about the new Consortium's progress, goals, and benefits in future issues of The X Resource.

If you have any questions about the new Consortium, please feel free to contact me: *abel@expo.lcs.mit.edu*, or call 617-253-8852.

BIOGRAPHICAL SKETCH OF LUTHER C. ABEL

Luther Abel is a twenty-year veteran of the computer software industry. For his entire career, Lu has been involved with sophisticated applications, primarily in the CAD/CAM field, employing computer graphics as their primary user interface. Lu has bachelor and masters degrees in electrical engineering from Rensselaer Polytechnic Institute and a PhD in computer science from the University of Illinois.

For the past two years, Lu has been a consultant specializing in engineering productivity, product development cycle and time-to-market speedup, and CAD/CAM tool selection and integration.

Prior to starting his consultancy, Lu was Corporate CAD Director at Data General where he revitalized DG's internal CAD support group, transforming it into a vital trusted partner in DG's engineering activities. He led the creation of a totally new product development environment for Data General which is among the most advanced at any computer vendor. Key elements of this included a shift from internally-developed tools running on mainframe computers to a mix of strategic-partner-provided purchased and internally developed software running on a very large workstation network.

Previously, Lu was Vice President of Engineering at Via Systems from 1985 to 1987. Via Systems was among the first to recognize a market shift in technical applications away from "turnkey systems" (which embraced both the application itself and a non-standard computer on which it ran) to software packages to run on the emerging standardized UNIX workstation. Under Lu's leadership, Via was the first vendor to develop a complete semiconductor design system running on Sun workstations.

Before joining Via, Lu was Product Development Director at Applicon, one of the pioneers of the CAD/CAM industry. Lu was responsible for products comprising over 50% of Applicon's revenue stream. While there, he personally led the specification and development of a new generation of VAX-based products to replace Applicon's earlier PDP-11 based product line.

From 1972 through 1981, Lu held a succession of increasingly responsible positions within Digital Equipment Corporation rising from individual contributor to senior manager in charge of Digital's internal CAD software development efforts. In addition to providing crucial CAD technology needed for every innovative product brought to market by Digital in the 1975-1985 timeframe (e.g., the DEC-20, Digital's first ECL computer, the VAX/750, Digital's first ASIC machine, and the VAX/8600 and /8800), Lu was instrumental in perceiving and driving the organizational changes needed to support an engineering clientele which grew tenfold, became increasingly diverse in technology, and dispersed from a single product development site to dozens distributed worldwide.

Lu has a BSEE from Rensselaer Polytechnic Institute and a PhD in Computer Science from the University of Illinois

FROM BOB SCHEIFLER

The expectation going into this process was that the Future Committee would make the selection, and have me ratify the selection before presenting the nomination to the membership at large. I worked actively with the Future Committee throughout the process, and I concur with their selection and their assessment: I give Lu my strong endorsement. Lu has already begun digging into the job, and I expect to bring him on shortly as a consultant to MIT so that he has a base to work from in creating the new organization.

FROM THE FUTURE COMMITTEE

At the Advisory Committee meeting of 24 September 1991, Bob Scheifler announced his intention to step down as Director of the X Consortium at the end of 1993 and return to doing research. At the same time, the MIT Laboratory for Computer Science then expressed its belief that Bob's departure would provide a good opportunity for the X Consortium to move out from underneath MIT's wing.

In response, the Future Committee was established to examine the various options before the Consortium and recommend a course of action. On 14 March 1992, we published our proposal to the membership that the X Consortium become an independent, not-for-profit corporation.

Since that proposal was sent out, we have actively been recruiting people for the position of President of the X Consortium. To help in our search, we interviewed several executive search organizations and finally chose to retain the firm of Christian & Timbers. Over the last 7 months we have examined more than a dozen candidates, judging them on a number of different criteria, including:

- Business skills; in order to succeed, the X Consortium must remain a viable organization, particularly during the transition out of MIT.

- Leadership; especially the ability to put together, represent, and promote the vision of where the X Window System should go over the next 5 years.

- Technical management skills; the ability to assemble and keep a high-caliber team.

- Technical background, particularly in dealing with computer software products

- Ability to learn quickly.

- Personality and the ability to build rapport with the membership.

The pool of candidates from which we made our selection was outstanding; many of them would have been able to do the job with distinction. However, we found one candidate to be particularly captivating, and whom we wish to present to you at this time.

The Future Committee is proud to announce its unanimous recommendation that Dr. Luther Abel of Procon Systems and formerly of Data General, Via Systems, Applicon, and Digital Equipment Corporation be selected to form and lead the new X Consortium.

Lu excels in all of the categories we were looking for. His views on the challenges and opportunities facing the X Consortium are insightful. He is outgoing, dynamic, inquisitive, and is committed to working closely with the membership on a continuing basis to determine how the X Consortium can continue to meet their needs and the needs of their customers. He has run substantial organizations and has repeatedly shown the ability to recruit and retain staffs of the highest caliber. He is honest and straightforward and has inspired deep loyalty in the people who have worked for him. He has delivered a number of products that have required both technical and marketing expertise. His presentation and communication skills are outstanding. Furthermore, he is very excited about the X Consortium, its mission and activities, and the prospect of taking over its helm.

We believe that Lu is the best choice for the position and that you will find him to be as engaging as we have. He has gained our trust and confidence that he will be able to pick up the reigns from Bob and successfully guide the X Consortium during this tumultuous time. We look forward to working with him and give him our strongest endorsement. We hope you will also.

Sincerely,

Bill Crane, chair, NCD (formerly SunSoft)
Vasudev Bhandarkar, Apple (formerly DEC)
Dave Cassing, Tektronix
Jim Fulton, NCD
Nelson Mills, Hewlett-Packard
Jeanne Smith, IBM

THE X USER:

XRDB AND SCREEN-SPECIFIC RESOURCES

Miles O'Neal

The R5 release of the X Window System included significant but mostly unnoticed enhancements to *xrdb* in the area of per-screen, or screen-specific, resources.

Prior to R5, all resources were placed on the RESOURCE_MANAGER property on the root window of screen 0. R5 still uses this property for global resources but adds the capability to use a SCREEN_RESOURCES property for each screen. *xrdb* places this property on the root window of any or all screens as specified by the *xrdb* command-line arguments. If no screens are specified, everything works as it did before R5.

Client code does not need to change to utilize this new capability. However, the client must be relinked with a library (such as R5 Xt) that reads the SCREEN_RESOURCES property.

Why would you need screen-dependent resources? I have run across two situations in which I needed this in my work.

The first is somewhat similar in concept to *xrdb*'s processing using the COLOR variable, but the execution is quite different. Just as some system configurations include a mono and a color screen, others include two color screens of different resolutions or depths. In this case, while red is probably recognizable as red on both screens, various shades of red may not be easily distinguished on a screen with fewer colors. Lower-resolution screens may require different fonts, line widths, and so on.

In the other case, color is used to allow the user to more easily identify what he or she is seeing. A subway monitoring system uses one screen per rail line, and the colors used for each screen match the line's colors (a Red Line and a Blue Line).

In either case, the solution is to use the new `-screen` option of the *xrdb* command. Unfortunately, the man page is not completely clear on the proper usage of this feature.

Miles O'Neal (meo@pencom.com) is a Senior Software Engineer at Pencom Software.

As part of its processing, *xrdb* invokes *cpp* (the C preprocessor) on its input. The *xrdb* man page mentions a number of variables *xrdb* defines for *cpp*, such as CLIENTHOST, COLOR, and CLASS. While these variables (or macros, as they are known in preprocessor parlance) could theoretically be used as parts of resource definitions, in practice these variables aren't very useful for this. Instead, *cpp* tests for the existence or values of these variables in order to decide what should be passed through to the resource database processing code in *xrdb*. Some of this is shown in my sample resource file included at the end of this article.

Unfortunately, *xrdb* does not define any screen-dependent resource variables. This would make complex resource files easier to manage by means of *cpp*'s conditional tests, such as #if and #ifdef. An example of how to get around this also appears in my sample resource file.

To set resources specific to screens 0 and 1 of display 0 on hostname, you could use the following commands (the file names are only suggestions):

```
% xrdb -load -screen -display hostname:0.0 .Xdefaults_0
% xrdb -load -screen -display hostname:0.1 .Xdefaults_1
```

After these commands are completed, any global (per-display) resources remain unchanged. The -screen -display hostname:display.screen arguments are all required to set or query screen-dependent resources. To examine screen-dependent resources, you use the same syntax as you normally would, with the addition of the preceding arguments, as follows:

```
% xrdb -query -screen -display hostname:0.0
```

This will show the screen-dependent resources for screen 0.

To see the resources set on all screens, you would simply type

```
% xrdb -query -screens
```

resulting in output similar to the following:

```
! screen-independent resources

! screen 0 resources
*RailLineColor: Red
*Text*Background: Pink

! screen 1 resources
*RailLineColor: Blue
*Text*Background: LightBlue
```

Likewise, you can specify -screens with the -load, -remove, or -merge options. This is used primarily with -merge to override settings without a complete reload or with -remove.

To see all resources (both screen-independent and screen-dependent resources), you specify the -all option (this is the default for the R5 version of *xrdb*). To see only screen-independent resources, you specify the -global option.

Note that using -all has no effect on a display with only one screen. This is because *xrdb* assumes that displays with one screen do not use screen-dependent resources. Accessing screen-dependent resources in a single-screen environment requires explicitly accessing that screen by means of the -screen and -display arguments of *xrdb*. You may find it easier to simply test for hostnames known to have single-screen displays, and handle them by using only screen-independent resources. Even in the single-screen case, if you specify screen-dependent resources, they will still have precedence over screen-independent resources.

To centralize my resources, I prefer to have everything that is loaded by *xrdb* handled through *.Xdefaults*. To easily utilize this configuration with screen-independent resources, I use the -D option of *xrdb*, which *xrdb* passes to *cpp* to define a variable. The following is similar to a set-up I used on a system with two color screens on one display—the first a 4-bit screen, and the second a 16-bit screen. (Note that I use both *cpp*-defined and *xrdb*-defined symbols, to better configure whichever system I'm on.)

.Xdefaults:

```
#ifdef SCREEN
# if SCREEN == 0
#    include "/u/meo/.Xdefaults_0"
# elif SCREEN == 1
#    include "/u/meo/.Xdefaults_1"
# endif
#else
        *DefaultFont: -*-courier-medium-r-normal--*-100-*-*-m-*-*-*
# include "/u/meo/app-defaults/XTerm"
# ifdef NeXT
        *WarningColor: Orange
        XTerm*Background: #000040
        XTerm*Foreground: White
# else
        *WarningColor: Red
        XTerm*Background: MidnightBlue
        XTerm*Foreground: Wheat
# endif
!
# if (SERVERHOST == hostname) && (CLIENTHOST == vulture)
#    include "/u/meo/app-defaults/LoginMgr"
# endif
#endif
```

.Xdefaults_0:

```
*RailLineColor: Red
! The following is because screen 0 has lower resolution
*DefaultFont: 9x15
```

.Xdefaults_1:

```
*RailLineColor: Blue
```

The following commands then appear in my *.xinitrc* and *.xsession* files:

```
% xrdb -merge ~/.Xdefaults
% xrdb -screen -display :0.0 -merge ~/.Xdefaults -DSCREEN=0
% xrdb -screen -display :0.1 -merge ~/.Xdefaults -DSCREEN=1
```

I link my *.xinitrc* and *.xsession* files so that they always have the same contents even though only one needs to be edited. This makes it easier to maintain them.

BEST OF NETNEWS

Edited by Marc Albert

This regular column contains articles that have appeared recently in the *comp.windows.x* Usenet discussion group. We have attempted to choose articles of wide interest and lasting value. The articles have been edited for publication. All authors have reviewed their postings and have had the opportunity to update them if necessary. We have attempted to give proper credit to the author of each article.

QUESTIONS ANSWERED IN THIS ISSUE

1. How can I check for the existence of an *app-defaults* file from my program?
2. Is it possible for a parent window to paint over its child windows?
3. Does X provide any statistics about server memory usage?
4. Is Xlib thread safe?
5. What are the advantages of using gadgets instead of widgets?
6. Why do I get unresolved externals for XtShellStrings and XtStrings?
7. Is it possible to determine how much screen space the Window Manager–supplied decorations will use?
8. Are there rules about the order in which widget resources are initialized?
9. Is there a way to associate some arbitrary data with a window?
10. How can I add support for *editres* in programs that don't use the Athena widget set?
11. How can I tell how many color cells are available?
12. Shouldn't a resource specification set in a resource file in a user's home directory always take priority over those in */usr/lib/X11/app-defaults?*

1. How can I check for the existence of an *app-defaults* file from my program?

>From: George Ross <*gdmr@dcs.ed.ac.uk*>

Define a Boolean application resource named *appDefaultsFileInstalled*, and set the default value to False in your code. Have your *app-defaults* resource file set *appDefaultsFileInstalled* to True. If you find, after you have done your XtGetApplication-Resources(), that the value of the resource is False, you can complain to the user.

2. Is it possible for a parent window to paint over its child windows?

>From: Gerard O'Driscoll <*gerard@dps.co.uk*>

Use a GC with the subwindow_mode attribute set to IncludeInferiors(). The default is ClipByChildren(). Beware that, if any of the children are of a depth different from that of the parent, this operation is undefined by the protocol.

3. Does X provide any statistics about server memory usage?

>From: der Mouse <*mouse@thunder.mcrcim.mcgill.edu*>

No. Even if you could get this information, the answer could be out of date before you get it (even if you grab the server, memory could be taken up by buffering user actions). You should just try to do whatever you want; a BadAlloc error is your indication that insufficient server memory is available.

4. Is Xlib thread safe?

>From: Stephen Gildea <*gildea@expo.lcs.mit.edu*>

No, the R5 Xlib is not thread safe—but it is being worked on. Consortium members will have a multithreaded version soon, and it will be part of X11R6.

5. What are the advantages of using gadgets instead of widgets?

>From: Adrian Nye <*adrian@ora.com*>

It is a case of memory versus network performance trade-off. Gadgets save both client and server memory. But memory is easily expandable while network performance is not, so if I were designing a toolkit I would at least make it possible to avoid using gadgets.

6. Why do I get unresolved externals for XtShellStrings and XtStrings?

>From: Michael Salmon <*etxmesa@eos.ericsson.se*>

They aren't functions; they are arrays of pointers to characters. The standard strings are defined either as string constants or as pointers into these arrays. The method used is determined by the XTSTRINGDEFINES setting. Your libraries were compiled with XTSTRINGDEFINES defined and your application with it undefined, so simply recompile one or the other. It is probably worth adding -DXTSTRINGDEFINES to your CFLAGS.

7. Is it possible to determine how much screen space the Window Manager–supplied decorations will use?

>From: Alan Frost <*alan@neocad.com*>

After your toplevel widget has been realized but not mapped (set `XtNmappedWhenManaged()` to False), get the x and y values and save them. Next, map the toplevel widget and monitor for `ConfigureNotify()` events on it. When you get the first one, it will be from the window manager. The window manager will have moved your toplevel widget to make room for its decorations. The x delta is a good value to use for the left, right, and bottom window manager decorations, and the y delta can be used for the top.

Since there is no "official" way to do this, it may not work properly with all window managers, but at least this method doesn't rely on knowing which window manager is running.

8. Are there rules about the order in which widget resources are initialized?

>From: Donna Converse <*converse@expo.lcs.mit.edu*>

The specification for `XtCreateWidget()` says that a widget's regular resources are initialized before a widget's constraint resources. Otherwise, no specific order is implied.

It would be better to place in the `initialize` method of the widget (and you have to write it anyway for the `set_values` method) some code that computes the value of the resource based on the value of the other resources. That is where this kind of computation is normally done. At the point that the widget's `initialize` method is called, you do know that all of the resource fields have been initialized.

9. Is there a way to associate some arbitrary data with a window?

>From: Tom LaStrange <*toml@boulder.ParcPlace.COM*>

One way is to place a property on the window. Accessing this data, however, is subject to round-trip performance considerations because the data is managed by the X server. If the data needs to be accessible only to your application, you can try `XSaveContext()`.

10. How can I add support for *editres* in programs that don't use the Athena widget set?

>From: Marc Albert <*marc@mvision.com*>

You can add support for *editres* to any Xt-based program if you simply add the following code fragments. You will also have to add the Xmu library to your link line.

```
#include <X11/Xmu/Editres.h>

XtAddEventHandler(TopLevelWidget, (EventMask)0, True,
    _XeditresCheckMessages, NULL);
```

11. How can I tell how many colorcells are available?

>From: der Mouse <*mouse@thunder.mcrcim.mcgill.edu*>

You can't. For one thing, it depends on exactly what colors you're allocating, because you may match colors that are already allocated and hence get an already allocated cell instead of a new one. Even if you rephrase it to ask "How many cells are unallocated?" there is no simple way to answer; you simply have to try it and see (unless you want to design and implement an extension, of course).

[Editor's note: You can write code that finds out how many unallocated cells there are, but it is time-consuming. You write a loop that attempts to allocate N colors,, where N is large, and then reduce N by using a binary search algorithm. Whenever you allocate colors successfully, you free those colorcells before the next attempt at a larger N. On an 8-plane system, this finds the exact number of free cells in 8 or fewer iterations, assuming the number of free cells isn't changing. The code for this was shown in THE X RESOURCE, Issue 0.]

12. Shouldn't a resource specification set in a resource file in a user's home directory always take priority over those in */usr/lib/X11/app-defaults*?

From: Antonio Freixas <*tonyf@ims.com*>

Remember that the order in which resource files are searched is relevant for duplicate resource entries only. One thing a lot of people forget is that if the following two resources are defined in two different X resource files, the first resource will always override the second, no matter in which order the files are read:

```
a.b.c:value1
a*c:   value2
```

I've gotten into the habit of using the following approach so that things are more likely to work the way I expect:

1. In a system resource file, omit the application instance and class names (e.g., `*foreground`).

2. In a personal resource file, precede each resource with the class name (e.g., `XTerm*-foreground`).

3. In the *.Xdefaults* file, precede each resource with the instance name (e.g., `xterm*-foreground`) except for resources that are intended to apply to *all* programs.

This scheme is not perfect, and there are times when it can't be followed, but it raises the odds of things working the way one expects. I think rule 1 should *always* be followed by anyone shipping a system resource file. This allows the program author to suggest a resource value (e.g., `*foreground:red`) and the user to override the value globally in the *.Xdefaults* file (e.g., `*foreground:blue`).

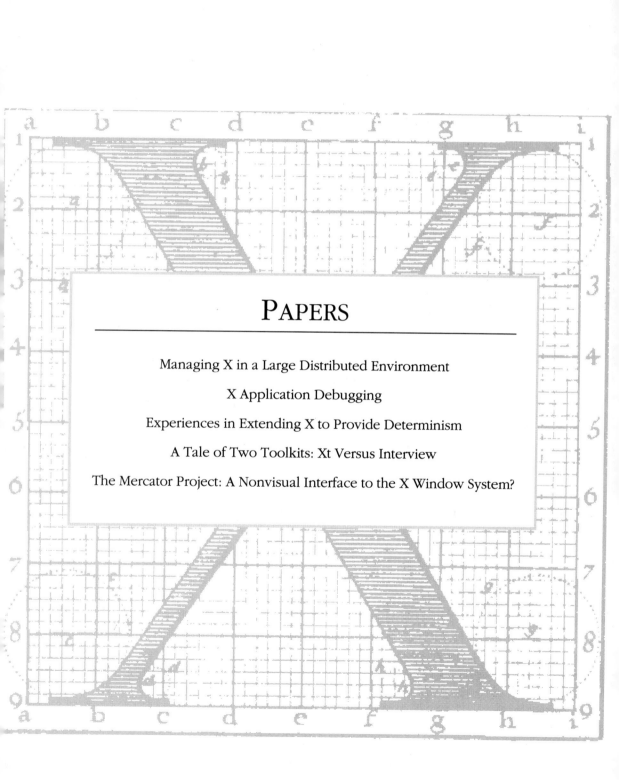

PAPERS

THE MERCATOR PROJECT:

A NONVISUAL INTERFACE TO THE X WINDOW SYSTEM

W. Keith Edwards, Elizabeth D. Mynatt, and Tom Rodriguez

ABSTRACT

This paper describes work to provide mappings between X-based graphical user interfaces and auditory interfaces. In our system, dubbed Mercator, this mapping is transparent to applications. The primary motivation for this work is to provide accessibility to graphical user interfaces for users who are blind or severely visually impaired. We describe the features of an auditory interface that simulates many of the characteristics of graphical interfaces. We then describe the architecture we have built to model and transform graphical interfaces. We present some of the difficulties encountered in building such a system on top of X. Finally, we conclude with some indications of future work.

Keith Edwards is a Research Assistant at the Georgia Tech Multimedia Computing Group. His research interests focus on computer-supported cooperative work. His email address is keith@cc.gatech.edu.

Beth Mynatt is a Research Scientist at Georgia Tech, where she manages the Multimedia Computing Group. Her interests include auditory interfaces and novel interaction techniques. Her email address is beth@cc.gatech.edu.

Tom Rodriguez is a Research Assistant at the Multimedia Computing Group. His interests include window systems and digital video. His email address is jack@cc.gatech.edu.

INTRODUCTION

A common design principle for building computer applications is to separate the design and implementation of the application functionality from the application interface. The reasons for this separation are clear. If the application interface or, more precisely, the presentation of the application interface is independent of the application behavior, then the interface can be easily modified to suit the needs of a wide range of users.

The graphical user interface is at this time an extremely common vehicle for presenting a human-computer interface. There are many times, however, when a graphical user interface is inappropriate or unusable. One example is when the task requires that the user's visual attention is directed somewhere other than at the computer screen. Another example is when the computer user is blind or visually-impaired. Unfortunately, graphical user interfaces, or GUIs, have disenfranchised this portion of the computing population. Presently, graphical user interfaces are all but completely inaccessible for computer users who are blind or severely visually-disabled [BBV90][Bux86][Yor89].

This critical problem has been recognized and addressed in recent legislation (Title 508 of the Rehabilitation Act of 1986, Americans with Disabilities Act of 1990) that mandates that computer suppliers ensure the accessibility of their systems and that employers must provide accessible equipment [Lad88]. The motivation for this legislation is clear. As more organizations move to a standard graphical environment, visually-impaired computer users may lose employment. Although this legislation has yet to be tested in the courts, both vendors and consumers of computer equipment and software are beginning to seriously address accessibility concerns.

Our work on this project began with a simple question: how could we provide access to X Window System applications for blind computer users? Historically, blind computer users had little trouble accessing standard ASCII terminals. The line-oriented textual output displayed on the screen was stored in the computer's framebuffer. An access program could simply copy the contents of the framebuffer to a speech synthesizer, a braille terminal, or a braille printer. Conversely, the contents of the framebuffer for a graphical interface are simple pixel values. To provide access to GUIs, it is necessary to intercept application output before it reaches the screen. This intercepted application output becomes the basis for an off-screen model of the application interface. The information in the off-screen model is then used to create alternative, accessible interfaces.

The goal of this work, called the Mercator[†] Project, is to provide transparent access to X applications for computer users who are blind or severely visually-impaired [ME92a][ME92b]. To achieve this goal, we need to solve two major problems. First, to provide transparent access to applications, we need to build a framework that will allow us

---

† Named for Gerhardus Mercator, a cartographer who devised a way of projecting the spherical Earth's surface onto a flat surface with straight-line bearings. The Mercator Projection is a mapping between a three-dimensional presentation and a two-dimensional presentation of the same information. The Mercator Environment provides a mapping from a graphical display to an auditory display of the same user interface.

to monitor, model, and translate graphical interfaces of X applications without modifying the applications. Second, given these application models, we need to develop a methodology for translating graphical interfaces into nonvisual interfaces.

In this paper, we describe the steps we have taken to solve these two problems. In the following section, we describe the design for the Mercator interface. We introduce the concept of audio GUIs and the abstract components of auditory interfaces. We also detail some of the techniques we are using to convey a range of interface attribute information using the auditory channel.

Next, we describe the architecture we have constructed to provide this interface transparently for X applications. We detail the requirements and goals of the system, the individual components of the architecture, and how those components interoperate to provide a translation of a graphical interface into an auditory interface.

AUDITORY INTERFACES

The primary human-interface design question to be addressed in this work is: given a model for a graphical application interface, what corresponding interface do we present for blind computer users? In this portion of the paper, we discuss the major design considerations for these audio user interfaces. We then describe the presentation of common interface objects such as buttons, windows, and menus, and detail the navigation paradigm for Mercator interfaces.

DESIGN CONSIDERATIONS

There are several design decisions we had to make when constructing our nonvisual interface. A major design question for building access systems for visually-impaired users is to what degree the new system will mimic the existing visual interface. At one extreme the system can model every aspect of the visual interface. The user could move a mouse over a screen and hear the objects announced as the cursor touches the object. In this type of system the user must contend with several characteristics of graphical systems that may be undesirable in an auditory presentation, such as mouse navigation and occluded windows. At the other extreme, the system could provide a completely different interface that bears little to no resemblance to the existing visual interface. For example, a menu-based graphical interface can be transformed into an auditory command line interface.

The primary question here is: what aspects of the graphical interface contribute to the user's model of the application and what aspects of the graphical interface are simply visual artifacts of its graphical presentation? Retaining the user's model of the application interface across presentations is necessary to support collaboration between sighted and nonsighted users. It is also important to remove visual artifacts of the graphical presentation that do not make sense in the auditory domain. For example, scrollbars serve two purposes in graphical interfaces. First they conserve limited screen real estate by presenting only a portion of a list. Second, they provide a mechanism for the user to quickly search the list. The first use of the scrollbar most likely does not need to be conveyed in the auditory interface, since there is no limited display real estate. The second use does need to be transferred to the auditory domain. But the movement of the scrollbar (up or down so many items) would need to be based on the auditory presentation of the scrollable object, not its visual presentation.

Essentially, we have chosen a compromise between the two extremes that we just outlined. To ensure compatibility between visual and nonvisual interfaces, we are translating the interface at the level of the interface objects that form the user's model of the application interface. For example, if the visual interface presents menus, dialog boxes, and pushbuttons, then the corresponding auditory interface will also present menus, dialog boxes, and pushbuttons. Only the presentation of the interface objects will vary.

Another design consideration is that of which nonvisual interface modality to use. The obvious choices are auditory and tactile. We are currently basing our design on previous work in auditory interfaces that has demonstrated that complex auditory interfaces are usable [BGB91][Edwa89]. Another factor that we considered is that a significant portion of people who are blind also suffer from diabetes, which may cause a reduction in their sensitivity to tactile stimuli [HTAP90]. Nevertheless, our system will eventually have tactile components as well. For example, a braille terminal provides an alternate means of conveying textual information—a means that is sometimes preferred to speech synthesis.

INTERFACE COMPONENTS

As stated in the preceding section, the auditory presentation will be based on the user's model of the application interface. This model will be composed of the objects that make up the graphical presentation. The constructs of the user's model can be thought of in terms of common interface objects such as menus, buttons, and dialog boxes, or in terms of the functions afforded by these objects, such as "selection from a set" or "containing heterogenous types of information." In X applications, these objects correspond roughly to widgets. There does not always exist a one-to-one mapping between graphical interface components and X widgets. For example, a menu is made up of many widgets, including a shell (a type of container), a geometry manager, and several types of buttons.

In Mercator, we call the objects in our auditory presentation *auditory interface components*, or AICs. The translation from graphical interface components to AICs occurs at the widget level. The Mercator Model Manager stores the widget hierarchy for the application interface and any attribute information associated with the widgets. Using a set of rules and widget templates, these widgets are combined to form abstract interface objects.

As with graphical interface components, there is not always a one-to-one mapping between X widgets and AICs. AICs may be composed of many widgets. Additionally, many visual aspects of widgets need not be modeled in AICs. For example, many widgets serve only to control screen layout of subwidgets. In an environment where there is no screen, there is no reason to model a widget that performs screen layout. For many widgets there *will* be a one-to-one mapping to AICs. As an example, pushbuttons (interface objects that perform a single function when activated) exist in both interface domains. In other cases, many widgets may map to a single AIC.

There are two types of information to convey for each AIC: the type of the AIC and the various attributes associated with the AIC. In our system, the type of the AIC is conveyed with an auditory icon. Auditory icons are sounds that are designed to trigger associations with everyday objects, just as graphical icons resemble everyday objects [Gav89]. This mapping is easy for interface components such as trashcan icons but is less straightforward for components such as menus and dialog boxes, which are abstract notions and have no innate sound associated with them. As an example of some of our auditory icons, touching a window sounds like tapping on a glass pane, searching through a menu creates a series of shutter sounds, a variety of push-button sounds are used for radio buttons, toggle buttons, and generic pushbutton AICs, and touching a text field sounds like a old-fashioned type-writer.

AICs can have many defining attributes. Most AICs have text labels that can be read by a speech synthesizer upon request. Many attributes can be conveyed by employing *filtears* to the auditory icon for that AIC. Filtears provide a just-noticeable, systematic manipulation of an auditory signal to convey information [LPC90][LC91]. Table 1 details how filtears can be used to convey some AIC attributes.

ATTRIBUTE	AIC	FILTEAR	DESCRIPTION
Selected	All buttons	Animation	Produces a livelier sound by accenting frequency variations.
Unavailable	All buttons	Muffled	A low-pass filter produces a duller sound.
Has submenu	Menu buttons	Inflection	Adding an upward inflection at the end of an auditory icon suggests more information.
Relative location	Lists, menus	Pitch	Map frequency (pitch) to relative location (high to low).
Complexity	Containers	Pitch, reverberation	Map frequency and reverberation to complexity. Low to large, complex AICs and high to small, simple AICs.

TABLE 1: *USING FILTERS TO CONVEY AIC ATTRIBUTES*

NAVIGATION PARADIGMS

The navigation paradigm for Mercator interfaces must support two main activities. First, it must allow the user to quickly "scan" the interface in the same way as sighted users visually scan a graphical interface. Second, it must allow the user to operate on the interface objects—pushbuttons, enter text, and so on.

In order to support both of these activities, the user must be able to quickly move through the interface in a structured manner. Standard mouse navigation is unsuitable, since the granularity of the movement is in terms of graphic pixels. Auditory navigation should have a much larger granularity, where each movement positions the user at a different auditory interface object. To support navigation from one AIC to another, we map the user interface into a tree structure that breaks down the user interface into smaller and smaller AICs. This tree structure is related to the application's widget hierarchy, but there is not a one-to-one mapping between the widget hierarchy and the interface tree structure. As discussed earlier, there is sometimes a many-to-one mapping between widgets and AICs. Additionally, an AIC may conceptually be a child of another AIC, but the widgets corresponding to these AICs may be unrelated. For example, a pushbutton may cause a dialog box to appear. These AICs are related (the dialog box is a child of the pushbutton), but the widget structure does not reflect the same relationship.

To navigate the user interface, the user simply traverses the interface tree structure. Currently, the numeric keypad is used to control navigation. Small jumps in the tree structure are controlled with the arrow keys. Other keys can be mapped to make large jumps in the tree structure. For example, one key on the numeric keypad moves the user to the top of the tree structure. It is worth noting that the existing application keyboard shortcuts should work within this structure as well.

Navigating the interface by means of these control mechanisms does not cause any actions to occur except making new AICs "visible." To cause a selection action to occur, the user must press the Enter key while on that object. This separation of control and navigation allows the user to safely scan the interface without activating interface controls.

ARCHITECTURAL OVERVIEW

The previous sections of this paper discussed the motivation and design for a nonvisual interface that is based on the semantic constructs in the original graphical interface of an application. We have also presented a keyboard-based navigation paradigm that allows users to scan and operate the interface. Now we discuss the architecture we have constructed to provide this alternative interface presentation and navigation. The component of the Mercator project that performs this translation of X-based graphical interfaces to auditory interfaces is called the Application Manager.

The Application Manager itself is composed of several components, and we discuss each of those components in turn. The remainder of this paper presents the tasks that must be performed by the Application Manager and the components of the system that accomplish these tasks.

CAPTURING INTERFACE INFORMATION

The most important technical obstacle that must be overcome in order to provide an alternative interface to existing applications is the problem of how to capture or retrieve information about the interfaces of applications as they are running. A system that provides an alternative interface to existing applications must ideally have access to the semantic properties of the original interface (for example, the types of objects in the interface and the structure of the interface), as well as the behavioral attributes of the interface ("clicking this button causes a dialog box to pop up"). Lower-level syntactic information may also be needed ("this text is in boldface; this button is red").

A number of possible approaches are possible to provide this level of information about application interfaces. One class of approaches involves changing the applications themselves, or changing the toolkits the applications are built with. By making direct modifications to application or toolkit code it is possible to introduce the mechanisms for nonvisual interfaces directly and efficiently into applications; the code that produces the nonvisual interface has available to it high-level information about the original interface and its behavior since it is "inside" the application. Of course, the drawback to this approach is that it requires modifications to applications and toolkits, and thus is not a transparent solution: it will not work with existing systems without recompilation (or at the least, relinking).

We have taken a different approach to the problem of information capture. Our system provides a nonvisual interface to existing, unmodified X applications by using an external process to capture information about the interface at runtime. Our approach has the advantage that it is completely transparent: client applications and the window server do not (and indeed *cannot*) know that our alternative interface system is in use. The chief drawback to our approach is that since our system exists outside of the applications and window system, it has only a limited amount of information available about the original graphical interfaces that it is attempting to translate.

This section presents the two mechanisms we are using to retrieve interface information from running applications. Both of these mechanisms operate transparently to both the applications and the window system.

PROTOCOL MONITORING

The most basic technique we use to capture interface information is to monitor the exchange of X protocol packets between the X server and clients. The component of the Mercator Application Manager that accomplishes this protocol monitoring is called the Protocol Interest Manager. See Figure 1 for a structural overview of the Application Manager.

The Protocol Interest Manager, or PIM, is in essence a *pseudo-server*. That is, it is a separate process that appears to clients to be an X Window System server. To the server itself, the PIM appears to be a client. Clients connect directly to the PIM in our system, and then the PIM establishes a surrogate connection to the "true" X server. Applications cannot distinguish the PIM from a real X server.

By tapping the connection between X clients and the server, the PIM is in a position to be notified of all changes in the interface: all window creations, maps and unmaps, text and graphics rendering, and size changes are represented in the protocol. The X protocol is the only mechanism for drawing to the screen (since the screen is owned by the X server itself in most cases), and thus it is essentially impossible to circumvent the X protocol to draw to the screen. The PIM is aware of any and all application output to the screen.

But even though monitoring the protocol can tell us in complete detail *what* has happened in the interface, it cannot tell us *why* something has happened. The information in the X protocol is extremely low-level and provides virtually no semantic clues as to the meaning of events in the protocol. For example, when a pushbutton is created, a sequence of protocol will be generated that creates and maps a window and draws some text into it. When the mouse is moved into the window, the border of the window is changed (highlighted). Based solely on the low-level information present in the X protocol, it would be extremely difficult, if not impossible, to derive the fact that the created object is a pushbutton.

EDITRES

To solve many of the problems that would be present if we relied on protocol monitoring alone, the Mercator Application Manager also makes use of the Editres protocol [Pet91]. The Editres protocol, introduced in X11R5, was designed to allow easy, interactive customization of applications. Editres provides facilities for querying running applications about their widget hierarchies, widget names and classes, and resources. This information is maintained by the Xt Intrinsics layer and is resident in the client itself; other than Editres there is no way for an external process to access this type of information in another client. The component of the Application Manager that implements the Editres protocol is called the Editres Manager (see Figure 1).

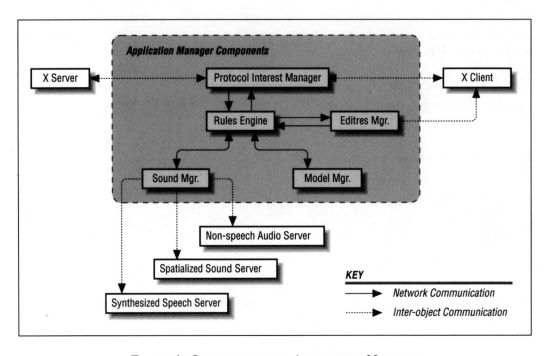

FIGURE 1: *OVERVIEW OF THE APPLICATION MANAGER*

We use the information that can be obtained through use of Editres to interpret the X protocol stream. In the preceding pushbutton example, when we detect by means of the protocol that a new window has been created and mapped, we generate an Editres query to the application to retrieve the widget hierarchy of the application. Contained in the reply is the name, class, widget ID, and window ID of all of the widgets and gadgets in the application. By matching the returned window IDs to the ID of the new window in the protocol, we can determine that indeed a pushbutton has just been created.

Combining the semantically high-level information from Editres with the all-inclusive protocol-based information gives us a good picture of what is going on inside the application interface. We are notified of changes in the state of the application by means of the X protocol, and can then use Editres to understand and interpret the meaning of the protocol in terms of high-level constructs such as buttons, menus, and scrollbars.

MODELING APPLICATIONS

Based on the information retrieved from an application, we must be able to synthesize a coherent model of the application's interface. We need to keep this interface representation locally so that we can have information about the interface available to us at all times without having to constantly poll the application to retrieve needed data. Also, we can store the interface information locally in a convenient format that can provide easy access to particular data as needed.

This model must provide a representation for not only the structure of the interface, but also appearance attributes, behavioral attributes, and semantic attributes. Our modeling techniques must be sufficiently flexible to support representing these (and possibly other) attributes of the applications that run in our environment.

Figure 2 provides a structural overview of the data structures we use to model application interfaces. The data structures shown here are controlled by the Model Manager component of the Application Manager. The Model Manager provides the programmatic interface to the interface representation for the rest of the Application Manager.

Since many clients may not implement Editres, the only information that is always *guaranteed* to be available to us is information present in the X protocol stream. The most important structural attribute of interfaces that is present in the protocol is the window hierarchy of the application. Thus our data structures provide a representation of this lowest common denominator of all X applications, the window. The Model Manager maintains a dictionary (key-value mapping) of Win objects that mirror the actual window hierarchy present on the display server. Win objects are our internal representation of relevant window attributes. This dictionary is updated automatically by the Protocol Interest Manager as windows are created, destroyed, or modified on the display server.

Of course, the problem with modeling windows alone is that, by themselves, windows are too low-level to be meaningful when trying to understand the semantics of an application's interface. To overcome some of the limitations of representing the window hierarchy alone,

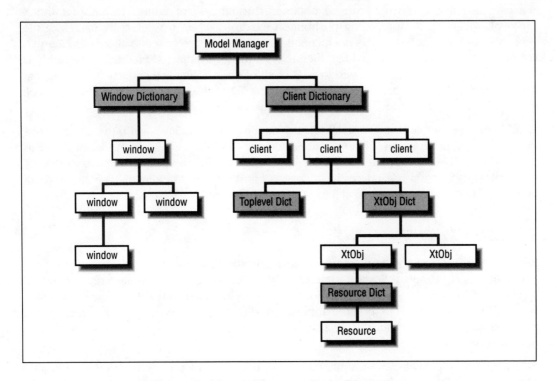

FIGURE 2: *MODEL MANAGER DATA STRUCTURES*

we also maintain a representation of the interface objects (widgets or gadgets) in the interface on a per-client basis. Note that this information is only available if the application in question understands the Editres protocol. The Model Manager keeps a list of Client objects, each of which represents one application running in the system. Client objects have unique identifiers based on the connection number of the application's protocol stream to the X server.

Client objects maintain the name and class of the application (sent as properties through the X protocol), and keep a dictionary that represents the interface object hierarchy of the application. Our internal representation for these interface objects is the XtObj class. Each XtObj instance models one widget or gadget in the application interface, and maintains information about parent and children object identifiers, the window ID of the object (if applicable), and any resources associated with the object. When XtObj instances are created, they also install "back-pointers" into the Model Manager's Win objects so that it is easy to locate a particular widget based on a window ID. As a convenience, Client objects also maintain a list of the top-level windows of their application.

There are a number of benefits to our approach to interface modeling. Because of the way our data structures are keyed, it is easy to determine which widget or widgets correspond to a window ID in the protocol stream. As an example, when we see a window being mapped in the protocol, we can use the window ID to determine the widget in the interface that has just been popped up. The information stored in the Model Manager allows us to interpret the X protocol to associate higher-level semantic meaning to occurrences in the interface.

APPLICATION OUTPUT

Once we have captured information about the interface of a running application, and stored that information in our off-screen model, we still must present that interface structure to the user in a meaningful manner. To create an auditory presentation of the interface representation stored in our off-screen model, we apply a set of translations to the interface representation. These translations produce a consistent auditory interface that is semantically similar to our stored representation of the application's original graphical interface. This section describes the particular mechanisms we use to accomplish this translation.

RULES ENGINE

The heart of the Mercator Applications Manager is the Rules Engine (see Figure 1). The Rules Engine takes as input the current state and structure of the interface, and any user input, and produces auditory output according to a set of translation rules. From a high-level standpoint, the Rules Engine has two responsibilities: to present the application interface to the user, and to respond to input from the user and generate controlling events to the application and possibly to the Application Manager itself. This section deals with the first goal, presenting the interface. See the later section titled "User Input" for a description of how we handle user input.

The Rules Engine is driven asynchronously by the Protocol Interest Manager, which taps the connection between the X client and the server. The Rules Engine informs the PIM of patterns in the X protocol that should cause control to be passed to the Rules Engine (that is, the Rules Engine expresses a *protocol interest*—hence the name of the Protocol Interest Manager). When the Rules Engine is "awakened" by the PIM, it examines the current state of the protocol and may fire one or more rules that may take any of a number of actions, including of course the production of auditory output.

The facilities available to translation rules are quite complex. For example, rules can stall the X protocol stream (that is, queue requests and events at the PIM for later delivery). Furthermore, rules can actually insert new requests or events into the protocol stream, change existing requests or events before they are delivered, or delete requests or events. When packets are inserted or deleted, the PIM rewrites later packets to ensure that sequence numbers remain consistent.

Rules can examine or update the interface representation stored in the Model Manager. They may also query applications and collect replies through Editres. Information returned by means of Editres is used to update the off-screen model of the interface's state.

Rules perform a number of functions in our system. Some rules are used only for "maintenance" of the interface representation. For example, when new windows are created, a rule fires that updates the window hierarchy representation in the Model Manager. If the request to create the window came from a client that understands the Editres protocol (an attribute that is stored in the Client objects in the Model Manager), then a second rule fires to retrieve an updated copy of the application's widget hierarchy in an attempt to match the newly created window to an actual widget.

Other rules actually create the auditory presentation of the interface. In the preceding window creation example above, a rule would also fire that would examine the state of the interface and the newly created object and generate some auditory output to inform the user that, for example, a dialog box has just been created.

Our rules are currently implemented in a stylized C++ predicate/action notation. Rule list traversal is quite fast: predicates are preprocessed and organized into hash tables based on protocol interest patterns (that form the basis of rule predicates). Thus, when a particular protocol sequence occurs, the system does not need to test the predicates of all rules, only the ones that have the specified protocol pattern as a predicate.

TEMPLATES

To obviate the need to install a large number of rules to deal with the different semantics of each individual widget in the interface, we have developed the notion of rule templates. Rule templates are sets of rules that are generated and installed automatically whenever a widget of a given class is created in the original interface. Templates provide consistency in the "hear and feel" of objects in Mercator interfaces.

For example, the rule template for widgets of the PushButton class may provide a set of rules to be fired whenever the PushButton instance is selected, desensitized, destroyed, and so forth. When the Rules Engine detects that a PushButton widget has been created, it generates and installs the rules specified in the rule template for this widget class. Thus, a set of routines is automatically associated with that particular PushButton instance that governs its interaction in the new interface. Rule templates provide a mechanism for ensuring standard behavior across all instances of a particular widget class with little work.

TEXT HANDLING

Computer interfaces are still comprised mostly of text. Early screen-reader systems for text-based interfaces (such as command line interfaces) accessed the screen contents by reading the ASCII codes stored in the display's framebuffer. In these systems, the spatial relationships between pieces of text on the screen was well defined, since the text was laid out in a grid. Because the basic display unit of GUIs is the pixel, capturing text in a GUI presents a different set of problems.

First, text drawn in a GUI is stored as pixels in the framebuffer, which are difficult to interpret as characters. Therefore the text must be captured before it is drawn. In Mercator this is accomplished by intercepting the text-drawing requests, ImageText and PolyText. These drawing requests are the only means of drawing text under X unless the application renders text itself, one pixel at a time. The text contained in these requests does not correspond directly to the text that will appear on the screen. All text under X is drawn using a font, with the characters acting as indices into the font. Thus the character "A" may be drawn as "A" in most fonts, but may appear as a special symbol in others. Thus we must track not only the text, but also the font it is drawn in.

Another problem with handling text in a GUI is that everything is drawn at pixel locations, so it is difficult to determine the effects of overwriting text with new text or graphics. Likewise, graphics requests are used to copy and erase text, so we need to accurately model the location and movement of text at the pixel level.

To solve these problems, our present implementation operates under two assumptions concerning the display of text. First, applications are not allowed to use proportional fonts to draw text. This constraint simplifies the bookkeeping for handling text, since we can assume that each character in a font takes up a fixed amount of space. This constraint is also easily configurable through the use of the resource database and enforceable by intercepting OpenFont requests.

Our second assumption is that all text in a window is drawn in the same font. This constraint eliminates some of the same bookkeeping needed for proportional fonts and appears to be a fairly valid assumption in general, though it is not always true.

Using these constraints we are able to model text similarly to the way text mapped on a terminal. Each window containing text is divided into a grid based on the text's font, and is stored and manipulated based on this grid. This model supports CopyArea and ClearArea requests since we can easily map the rectangular coordinates supplied in these requests.

The assumptions we made for handling text were acceptable for our prototype system, but the use of proportional fonts and the mixing of fonts are important issues that must be resolved in future systems.

SOUND SERVERS

As mentioned earlier, output to the user is generated by the specific rules fired by the Rules Engine. When fired, rules can invoke methods on the Sound Manager object (see Figure 1), which then generates the specified auditory output. The Sound Manager provides a single programmatic interface to the various sound resources available on our platform.

Currently, we use three types of sound output: speech, simple nonspeech audio, and high-quality spatialized (3-D) sound. Each type of sound output is generated by different hardware, and thus for each type there is a separate server process that regulates access to the sound hardware. These servers support access by means of multiple processes to workstation sound resources and allow sound hardware to reside on other machines across a network. See the later section titled "Status" for more details on the particulars of these servers.

USER INPUT

In addition to presenting application interfaces in a nonvisual mode, the Application Manager is responsible for processing user input to both the applications and the Application Manager itself. In essence, the Application Manager must *run* the existing application based on user input in the new interface. This section presents the mechanisms used for user input.

THE NOTION OF CONTEXT

The Application Manager maintains the notion of the user's *current context* in the environment as a construct to support navigation. The current context is defined as the application the user is currently working in, and a particular widget within that application where the user is currently "located." Users navigate through applications by changing their current context and by operating widgets at their current location. The Application Manager effects changes in context by actually warping the mouse pointer to the desired location in response to user input. We warp the pointer to ensure that applications in our environment behave exactly as they would in a visual environment if the user moved the mouse pointer to a new widget.

KEYBOARD INPUT

Currently, all input to the system is through the keyboard. Hence, since X "owns" the keyboard, all input to the system comes through the X server. It is the task of the Application Manager to translate keyboard input into appropriate events (including possibly mouse events) and routing those new events to the appropriate applications as a means of control. The Application Manager must also detect *metacontrols*—that is, input designated for the Application Manager itself, rather than one of the applications running on the system.

There are some potential problems with input to the Application Manager that are related to the fact that all input to the system comes through the X server. The primary problem is that not all widgets solicit keyboard-related events and, in general, if a particular widget does not solicit a certain event type, the server will never generate that event. This implies that some widgets will not be "navigable." That is, once the current context has changed to a widget that is not soliciting keyboard input, no further keyboard events will be generated from the server and it will be impossible to move out of that widget.

To work around this problem we have a set of rules that instruct the protocol interest manager to modify the X protocol stream in certain ways. First, whenever a CreateWindow request is generated, we intercept and modify the request to ensure that the newly created window has an event mask attribute that will cause keyboard events to be generated. Second, we monitor the protocol for ChangeWindowAttribute requests, and modify these requests if necessary to ensure that a client does not "turn off" solicitation for keyboard events at some later time. The Application Manager stores the "natural" state of event solicitation in the Model Manager, so that extraneous key-presses are never sent to windows that are not supposed to receive keyboard input. This approach seems to work quite well in practice.

Of course, not all input is directed to the Application Manager. Some input is intended for the applications themselves. Since the PIM has full control over the X protocol stream, we can simply remove events that are intended for the Application Manager. Thus, the "reserved" keys that are used for navigation are never seen by applications. Other keyboard events are passed through to the applications unmodified. Note that under our approach any standard application keyboard accelerators should continue to work.

We are currently beginning work on using other input streams (such as voice) that do not have to travel through the X server. We feel that the use of multiple input sources will greatly improve the human-computer bandwidth of the interface. We are also beginning to investigate the use of the X Input Extension as a means of accepting input from novel input devices.

BYPASSING UNWANTED OBJECTS

The concept of the user's context is maintained by keeping a pointer to the user's position in the application's widget hierarchy, which is stored in the off-screen model by the Model Manager. The user navigates the application interface by moving through this tree structure. But the granularity of the user's movements is in terms of interface objects, not X widgets. For this reason, many of the X widgets in the tree structure are skipped during the traversal process. The strategy is to place the user in the most specific widget that corresponds to the current interface object.

To bypass widgets that the user does not need to be aware of, we have marked various classes of widgets as not navigable by the Model Manager. Current marked classes are Core, Viewport, Grip, and Transient. As navigation input from the user is processed, the user's position is moved one step in the tree (left, right, up, and down). If the new position is at a class marked as not navigable, then the navigation request is propagated another step. The direction for the next step is dependent on whether the current object has siblings and/or children in the tree structure.

This approach does not allow us to bypass all the widgets we would like to avoid. Since our navigation is still based on the full widget hierarchy, there may be widgets that are critical to the overall tree structure that cannot be ignored. One example is a widget that has both siblings and children. Currently, it is not possible to navigate around such a widget in a systematic manner and not miss other widgets. We are exploring new algorithms to allow more flexibility in navigating these structures.

CAVEATS

There are a number of weaknesses in our current system. This section explores some of the more important of these weaknesses and provides some insight into various solutions we are attempting.

EDITRES

The Editres protocol was designed to allow easy customization of X applications. As such, it provides requests to get the widget hierarchy of an application, to query the names and types of resources in widget classes, and to change the values of resources in particular widgets. While these requests may support simple customization of applications, they are insufficient for Mercator because they do not provide a way to query the value of resources.

Widgets are sometimes used to implement several different interface objects and are configured based on the values of resources. For example, the XmRowColumn widget in the Motif toolkit may be used as a popup menu, a pulldown menu, an option menu, a menu bar, or a generic work area. This information is contained in the XmNrowColumnType resource. While we might be able to infer the capacity that the XmRowColumn was acting in, the information is directly available in the widget's resources. Because of the potential power of a GetValues request, we decided to extend Editres to support it, with the hope that the Editres supplied by the X Consortium will eventually support a similar request.

Another limitation of Editres that is related to its original design as a customization protocol is that it only supports polling. The information that Editres returns is valid only at the moment that it is sent to the Editres client. Changes in the widget hierarchy are not reported back to the Editres clients as they happen. Due to this limitation, we are required to watch for CreateWindow requests in the protocol stream and then request Editres to resend the widget hierarchy. This scenario exacerbates our flow-control problems (see the later subsection titled "Deadlock Potential") and results in extraneous requests, since there is no way to determine when the interface has stabilized.

Additionally, Editres uses ClientMessages and the selection mechanism to transmit requests and replies. While this transport mechanism is acceptable for a protocol intended for customization, it creates problems when it is used to gather information for an interactive application like Mercator. The selection mechanism is a synchronous, multistage protocol that unnecessarily increases the implementation complexity of Mercator and degrades interactive performance because of the transmission overhead. We were unable to address this problem without significantly modifying EditRes.

WIDGET SET DEPENDENCIES

There are a number of widget-set dependencies in Mercator. Such dependencies exist because Editres returns widget class names and resource names that are particular to the widget set the application is written with. The rules in Mercator must look for and recognize this widget set-specific information to know how to treat particular widgets. Unfortunately such dependencies will probably exist in any system similar to Mercator.

DEADLOCK POTENTIAL

There are some interesting potential deadlock conditions that we take care to avoid in the Application Manager architecture. Since the entire system is driven by the protocol interest manager, the thread of control must reside within the PIM when the Application Manager is "inactive."

Thus, whenever rule execution terminates, control is passed back to the PIM where the system blocks until either (1) some X request or event traffic is generated, or (2) some other user input takes place that the PIM has been instructed to monitor. Control must be returned to the PIM because when the PIM is not executing the X protocol stream is effectively stalled.

This behavior of blocking the protocol stream can cause several problems. The most common problem relates to the use of Editres. Editres requests are asynchronous. This means that the Application Manager transmits an Editres query and then, at some unspecified point in the future, the application returns the result of the query. The problem is that the Editres protocol is based on the X protocol (specifically, the selection mechanism), and thus Editres communication must proceed through the PIM like all X traffic.

A deadlock condition will arise if a rule instructs the Editres Manager to send a request and then blocks waiting on the reply, rather than returning control to the PIM. If control is not returned to the PIM, then the connection between the client and server is blocked and the Editres request is never sent. Obviously in this case a reply is never generated, so the Application Manager hangs forever, waiting for a reply that will never come.

This situation is an example of a general problem, in which various components of the Application Manager need to generate X traffic that will produce a response. (The selection protocol is one example of this, as are all round-trip requests generated by the Application Manager.) Care must be taken that the operation is separated into two phases: an initiating phase, and an action phase that is invoked when the reply returns.

We have constructed in the Application Manager a callback mechanism that can be used by rules when they would otherwise block waiting on communication. One unfortunate consequence of the wide use of callbacks is that the control flow in the Application Manager is rather complex. Often, a rule must be split across several chained callbacks because the rule initiates several round-trip requests or Editres queries.

LIMITATIONS OF RULES

Currently, it is difficult to modify or create new rules in our system. Since the rules are actually coded into the system, a knowledge of C++ is required at a minimum. Perhaps even more constraining is the fact that a significant amount of knowledge of the implementation of the Application Manager and X itself is required to create new rules. This is because rules must work with information stored in other parts of the Application Manager (such as the Model Manager), generate Editres requests, and perhaps even modify the X protocol stream. There is a great need for a higher-level, abstract representation of rules and the facilities available to rules to allow for easier experimentation and customization of interfaces.

FUTURE DIRECTIONS

This section details our future plans for the Mercator system.

GENERALIZE INPUT AND OUTPUT

In the current implementation of Mercator, user input and system output are directly specified in the system's translation rules. That is, the particular input syntax and modalities that
are required to control either the Application Manager or applications are hardcoded into
the Application Manager itself. Similarly, the syntax and modalities of output are hardcoded
into the Application Manager itself.

We are investigating a more flexible I/O system in which the translation rules would operate
on abstract input and output tokens. Separate input and output management systems would
govern mapping these abstract tokens into whatever particular syntax and modality the user
desires.

Such a system would allow much more flexible customization of the nonvisual interface
according to user preferences. For example, users could "remap" the output mechanics to
change the presentation of a dialog box to speech output, nonspeech audio output, or even
tactile output on a braille printer. Similarly, users could customize the system to support
different, perhaps overlapping, modalities for input. Speech, keyboard, and trackball input
could all be used as application input according to users' specifications.

EXTERNALIZATION OF RULES AND WIDGET DESCRIPTIONS

Our specification of translation rules and widget set-dependent class and resource names
are currently hardcoded into the Application Manager. The rules in our system are
expressed in a stylized C++ predicate/action notation by the system implementors. We are
working on an externalized rules representation that will be read in and parsed at runtime
by the Application Manager. This system will allow far easier customization of the interface
by both the developers and users of the system.

We are exploring the possibility of creating an externalized representation of any widget set-
specific information that would be used by the Mercator rules. This would allow us to more
easily support different widget sets and customize support for our current widget sets.

XT-BASED PROTOCOL

One of the goals of our system was to explore the quality of nonvisual interfaces that could
be produced from X applications using a completely external (outside the application)
approach. While our system works, it is quite complex and has some weaknesses (which
we described in the "Caveats" section of this paper). The major limitations of our current
system result from two basic properties of our information capture approach: (1) the X
protocol is so low-level that it is difficult both to monitor and to create rules that express

constructs in terms of the protocol, and (2) Editres was simply not designed for the task we are applying it to.

While we do get fairly good results from our current implementation, we are beginning to explore modifications to the Xt Intrinsics layer that would allow an external process to present an alternative interface to any Xt-based application, without requiring a complex protocol monitoring system. The modifications would consist of hooks into Xt that would allow an external process to communicate directly with the Xt layer of an application. This new Xt-based protocol would differ from Editres in several respects. Most importantly, it would be able to provide resource values to clients, and would support asynchronous notification of events in the interface (to obviate the need to constantly poll the application). Unlike Editres, the new protocol would also allow controlling input to be delivered to the application.

We feel that such a protocol, specifically designed for the task of providing alternative interfaces to X applications, would provide a greater degree of semantic information about the workings and structure of application interfaces than our current solution, and would be much easier to construct and modify.

The mechanisms built for such a system would have a great number of other applications as well. For example, since the protocol would allow another process to drive an X application, it would be possible to construct harnesses that would allow scripting or automated testing of graphical applications, much as it is possible to drive character-based applications programmatically in many systems now. A broadening of the goals of Mercator would allow "retargeting" of application interfaces to virtually any new modality, including speech (perhaps to allow interactive application use over a telephone), or would even provide a different look-and-feel in the 2-D graphical domain (for example, to translate a Motif application to an OPEN LOOK application "on the fly").

STATUS

The components of the Application Manager are implemented as C++ objects; the current implementation is approximately 12,000 lines of code. Our prototype runs on the Sun SPARCstation. The three audio servers discussed in this paper have been implemented as Remote Procedure Call (RPC) services, with C++ wrappers around the RPC interfaces.

We currently support two separate synthesized speech servers. One supports the DECtalk hardware; the other provides software-based synthesis. Each supports multiple user-definable voices. The nonspeech audio server controls access to the built-in workstation sound hardware (*/dev/audio* on the SPARCstation in our case), and provides prioritized access and dynamic mixing of audio data. The spatialized sound server currently runs on either a NeXT workstation or an Ariel DSP-equipped Sun SPARCstation. (Both systems are based on the Motorola 56001 digital signal processor.) The SPARC-based system supports spatialization of multiple channels in real time [Bur92a][Bur92b].

Currently, all of the Application Manager components except for the various sound servers execute as a single thread of control in the same address space. We are investigating whether a multithreaded approach would yield significant performance benefits and better code structuring.

Due to the widget-set dependencies discussed earlier in the "Caveats," our current implementation supports only the Athena widget set. We are investigating support for OLIT and Motif and possibly other non-intrinsics-based X toolkits.

ACKNOWLEDGMENTS

The Mercator Project is a joint effort by the Multimedia Computing Group (a part of the Graphics, Visualization, & Usability Center of Georgia Tech) and the Center for Rehabilitation Technology. We would like to thank John Goldthwaite of the CRT.

This work has been sponsored by the NASA Marshall Space Flight Center (Research Grant NAG8-194) and Sun Microsystems Laboratories. We would like to thank our technical contacts at these organizations—Gerry Higgins and Earl Johnson, respectively.

Also, a number of people have contributed a substantial amount of time and energy to the development of Mercator; without their hard work this system would not have been possible. We would like to thank Dave Burgess and Ian Smith in particular.

REFERENCES

[BBV90]L.H. Boyd, W.L. Boyd, and G.C. Vanderheiden. "The Graphical User Interface: Crisis, Danger and Opportunity." *Journal of Visual Impairment and Blindness*, pp. 496-502, December 1990.

[BGB91]Bill Buxton, Bill Gaver, and Sara Bly. "The Use of Non-speech Audio at the Interface." Tutorial presented at the ACM Conference on Computer-Human Interaction. New Orleans, 1991.

[Bur92a]David Burgess. "Real-Time Audio Spatialization with Inexpensive Hardware." In *Proceedings of International Conference on Signal Processing Applications and Technology.* Boston, MA, 1992.

[Bur92b]David Burgess. "Low Cost Sound Spatialization." *Proceedings of ACM Symposium on User Interface Software and Technology*, UIST'92, November 1992.

[Bux86]William Buxton. "Human Interface Design and the Handicapped User." *Proceedings of ACM Conference on Computer-Human Interaction*, CHI'86, pp. 291-297, 1986.

[Edwa89]Alistair D. N. Edwards. "Modeling Blind User's Interactions with an Auditory Computer Interface." *International Journal of Man-Machine Studies*, pp 575-589, 1989.

[Gav89]William W. Gaver. "The Sonicfinder: An Interface that uses Auditory Icons." *Human Computer Interaction*, 4:67-94, 1989.

[HTAP90]HumanWare, Artic Technologies, ADHOC, and The Reader Project. "Making Good Decisions on Technology: Access Solutions for Blindness and Low Vision." Industry Experts Panel Discussion, in Closing the Gap Conference, October 1990.

[Lad88]Richard E. Ladner. Public law 99-506, section 508, "Electronic Equipment Accessibility for Disabled Workers." *Proceedings of ACM Conference on Computer-Human Interaction*, CHI'88, pp. 219-222, 1988.

[LC91]Lester F. Ludwig and Michael Cohen. "Multidimensional Audio Window Management." *International Journal of Man-Machine Studies*, 34:3, pp. 319-336, March 1991.

[LPC90]Lester F. Ludwig, Natalio Pincever, and Michael Cohen. "Extending the Notion of a Window System to Audio." *Computer*, pp. 66-72, August 1990.

[ME92a]Elizabeth Mynatt and W. Keith Edwards. "The Mercator Environment: A Nonvisual Interface to X Windows and Unix Workstations." GVU Technical Report GIT-GVU-92-05. February 1992.

[ME92b]Elizabeth Mynatt and W. Keith Edwards. "Mapping GUIs to Auditory Interfaces." In Proceedings of ACM Symposium on User Interface Software and Technology, UIST'92, 1992.

[Pet91]Chris D. Peterson. "Editres-A Graphical Resource Editor for X Toolkit Applications." In *Proceedings of the Fifth Annual X Technical Conference*. Boston, MA, January 1991.

[Yor89]Bryant W. York, editor. *Final Report of the Boston University Workshop on Computers and Persons with Disabilities*, 1989.

MANAGING X IN A LARGE DISTRIBUTED ENVIRONMENT

George D. M. Ross

ABSTRACT

The Department of Computer Science at the University of Edinburgh operates a distributed computing network supporting over 1000 registered users
on about 300 assorted workstations and X terminals. This paper describes
how our X start-up scripts, resource-handling mechanisms, and the
window manager combine to provide an environment that meets the needs
of even the most naive of these users, while being easily managed and able
to be tailored to suit both course requirements and individual preferences.

*George D. M. Ross (gdmr@dcs.ed.ac.uk) is Senior Computing Officer in the Department of Computer Science,
University of Edinburgh, Scotland. He can be reached at the Department of Computer Science, University of Edin-
burgh, Kings Buildings, Mayfield Road, Edinburgh EH9 3JZ, Scotland. This paper is based on a talk given at the
European X User Group's 1992 conference, held at Brunel University, Uxbridge, West London in September 1992.*

INTRODUCTION

The Department of Computer Science at the University of Edinburgh supports over 1000 registered users, ranging in ability from complete beginners to sophisticated and experienced programmers, on nearly 300 assorted workstations and X terminals. Only a very few actually write any X code; the vast majority are end-users of X-based applications or are those who simply find a window system a useful productivity aid.

A variety of hardware is used at the department, including Sun-4 workstations, compute-servers and multiuser machines; Sun-3 workstations and X terminals; HP 300-series workstations; HP 700/X X terminals; some NCD X terminals; and several DEC compute-servers. In addition, we use a number of special-purpose machines operated by the central Computing Services and by other departments.

As far as possible, we provide a uniform view of the global file system from all our machines. Users' home directories are automounted on all systems, while local binaries, including those for X, are replicated on some 20 main fileservers and a dozen or so local disc caches, each of which is automatically updated nightly from a central master copy. (The details of the mechanism by which this is done are discussed in the paper and technical notes listed in the "References" section at the end of this paper.) Users can therefore log in to any workstation or terminal on the department's network and find more or less the same environment available.

The environment described here was first put together about three years ago, based on X11R3, although parts of it existed in prototype form before that.

X SOFTWARE

Where possible, we use the MIT X distribution rather than the versions bundled by the manufacturers. We have the MIT core clients and libraries installed on all architectures, with the R5 server used on all Sun machines, including those transformed into X terminals, and the R4 server used on the HP 300-series workstations. (Our compute-servers and special-purpose machines are generally operated headless.) There were several reasons for this decision:

- It results in a consistent set-up across platforms. This has benefits for both application writer and X maintainer, as utilities, libraries, and configuration files are always found in the same locations.

- Building from source makes it possible to conform to local conventions regarding the location of binaries, data, and configuration files. Common automatic procedures then apply.

- Server and library security hooks are available in a uniform fashion.

- New library features and server extensions are available more quickly than would be the case if manufacturers' own servers and libraries were used. Nonstandard server extensions can be incorporated as required.

- Libraries and (Sun) servers can be kept at the latest revision level.

There are, of course, cases in which a manufacturer's version might be "better" than the MIT distribution. For example, it might be faster on a platform, or it might have a useful extension such as Display PostScript or a more fully developed PEX. However, we have to weigh the support cost that is generally incurred by having to install copies on fileservers individually (or by adapting the software to our automatic distribution system) and any additional tailoring of our scripts against the benefits of the additional features provided by the particular non-MIT implementation, with the cut-off point varying according to the needs of the department at the time and the actual functionality provided by the version in question. We might also consider making the package available with a lower level of support such as with fewer fonts or a reduced level of security.

We operate an automatic nightly update procedure, by which most of our locally built software, and X in particular, is distributed from one master NFS server to (currently) about 20 slave servers. This server carries both architecture-specific and shared nonspecific master copies of all the local file systems. Overnight the slave servers compare their copies against the master, updating themselves as appropriate with the previous day's changes. (The details of how this is done are described in the paper and technical notes listed in the "References" section at the end of this paper.)

Installing new X clients, libraries, or other software consists therefore of building the particular package and then copying the relevant files to the architecture-specific and shared nonspecific master file systems. From there they propagate overnight to the slave NFS servers. We have set up our *site.def* X configuration file so as to simplify this procedure for *imake*-generated *Makefiles*, including the core MIT distribution and most contributed clients. Unfortunately, the R5 configuration process assumes that the path by which a file is installed is the same as the path by which it will eventually be used, which is not true in our case. We currently solve this problem by using a modified version of the *install* utility, which knows that paths of the form

        /usr/local/bin/...

should be transformed to

        /export/local/arch/bin/...

i.e., on the master copy of the file system, and similarly for *lib* and *etc*, and that

        /usr/local/share/...

should be transformed to

        /export/local/share/...

We really should also have a similarly modified version of *ranlib*, but new libraries are installed infrequently enough that its absence has been only a minor annoyance. When the files propagate to the slave servers, the transformation is undone again and the files end up where the *site.def* said they should.

In addition to the core MIT distribution, we have a considerable amount of contributed and commercial X software installed. With the exception of our DEC compute-servers, which are not used as general-purpose machines, this software is installed on as many platforms as it will build for, so as to maintain as uniform a user environment as possible.

THE USER ENVIRONMENT

Our user population is generally not interested in X configuration details, though a minority do require the ability to tailor almost every aspect of the environment. Our scripts and configuration files therefore supply suitable defaults at all stages during a session's initialization. These defaults can be modified on a group basis to suit particular courses, while experienced individual users are able to augment or bypass both the system-wide and group-specific defaults.

The mechanism by which this is done has been made as unobtrusive as possible. In particular, the system and group defaults require no files to be present in a user's home directories in order to take effect. This is for two reasons:

- As students proceed from one course to another, and indeed as courses are revised, the default resources, applications, and menus may change. It is much easier to edit one central file than it is to devise a script to edit files in users' own directories, particularly when those files may have been mangled in unpredictable ways.

- Naive users (and supposedly sophisticated ones too!) have been known to break their environment by editing or deleting files in their home directories that they do not recognize. It is safer not to have such files visible in the first place.

At the same time, we have tried to preserve compatibility with existing practice as far as possible, both for the benefit of users arriving with experience of X from elsewhere, and for those following suggestions in books or instructions provided with some packages.

COMMON START-UP FUNCTIONS

X session initialization is complicated somewhat by the need to support both *xdm* and shell-level start-up scripts. It is not an option for us to use *xdm* everywhere, as some users and courses require access to other window systems or directly into raw framebuffers.

It is also desirable to preserve as much commonality as possible in the start-up scripts, both to provide maintenance and to minimize the amount of effort required to tailor a user's environment. In particular, it is not acceptable for the user to require one set of configuration files when starting an X session using *xdm* and a different set when starting from a shell command prompt.

We have therefore factored out most of the required functionality into a shared session script that is called by small shell- and *xdm*-specific scripts. This common script

- tidies up the DISPLAY variable;
- loads any available local fonts;
- enables host-based authority-checking for the servers that don't understand mit-magic-cookie-1;
- loads the resource database;
- tidies up the key mapping for some keyboards;
- runs the user's preferred set of clients, or those defined for the user's group, or the global default set;
- opens the console window, if appropriate; and, finally,
- runs the window manager[†] as the distinguished session-defining client.

The mechanism used to load local fonts is quite simple: any subdirectories of <LibDir>/-*fonts.local* are assumed to be font directories and are appended to the font path.

THE RESOURCE DATABASE

xrdb is used to load the resource database in four steps:

1. A handful of "required" resources are loaded, which for some reason cannot go into the app-default files (for example, they may be dependent on the screen dimensions) but which should not easily be overridden by the user.
2. The remainder of the global default resources are merged.
3. Any group-specific resources are merged.
4. The contents of the user's *.Xdefaults* and *.Xresources* files, if they exist, are merged.

This provides an easy way for system managers, course organizers, and users to modify the defaults, either for personal preference or as instructed in the documentation for specific packages. Merging in the user's own resource files at the end is an upwardly compatible extension to the way these are usually handled.

Alternatively, the user may bypass steps 2 and 3 completely, but is then responsible, of course, for tracking any modifications to the system and group defaults. The session script checks for the existence of an *.Xdefaults-load* file in the user's home directory, and if one is found it is merged in place of the usual defaults. (The name is somewhat unsatisfactory but was chosen to reflect the actions of *xrdb*'s *−load* option.)

---

† *twm* by default, though another window manager, or indeed any X client such as *xterm* or *xquitbutton*, can be used by setting the XWM environment variable in the user's own *.x11rc* file.

Defining global defaults in this way has several advantages over modifying the app-defaults files of applications:

- iIt makes screen-specific tailoring easier than when the "customization" mechanism is used, particularly when several combinations of depths and sizes are involved.

- It separates local preferences from the definitions required for applications to run properly. It is also clearer for users who might want to further tailor an application's appearance, so that changes are less likely to be lost when new versions are installed.

- Group-specific defaults can be defined more easily and reliably than would be the case if they had to be conditionally included in a global file or, worse, incorporated through the "customization" mechanism.

SPECIFIC START-UP SCRIPTS

The start-up script called by the user from the shell level to start the X session does several things:

- It decides which X server to run, based on host architecture and framebuffer availability.

- It generates the "cookies" for the authorization mechanism.

- It inserts the X-specific directories into the user's PATH and LD_LIBRARY_PATH.

- It runs *xinit* by using the chosen server and common session script.

- It resets the keyboard and clears the screen when *xinit* has terminated.

xdm-specific start-up is complicated by the requirement that the resulting environment be the same as that obtained from a shell-level start-up. The particular problem is that simply modifying the user's PATH and LD_LIBRARY_PATH and then running the session script means that the user's default shell is never run as a login shell. As a result, the user's once-only login-time initialization does not take place. It is not desirable to require users to place all shell initialization in the "every time" rc-files, as this would both unnecessarily complicate these files and penalize the majority of shell start-ups, and in any case it would run counter to existing practice and documentation. Furthermore, it is not sufficient to have *xterm* clients run login shells, as other clients will still have an incomplete environment; in particular, the window manager and any clients started from its menus will not have a full environment defined.

Our solution to this problem is to have *xdm* run the user's favorite shell as a login shell, thus establishing the correct environment. This shell is given a one-line script as its input, whose sole purpose is to *exec* another script to perform the *xdm*-specific processing before running the common session script. The reason for this rather convoluted method is that, although most of our users have *bash* as their default shell, there are still a few using *csh* variants with a different syntax for environment variables and I/O redirection. Fortunately, the Bourne shell and C shell *exec* commands are sufficiently similar that a common script containing only this is acceptable to both. The script that is finally run can, of course, use the shell of its choice.

WINDOW MANAGERS

Our standard window manager is a slightly modified *twm*, with similarly modified versions of *vtwm* and *tvtwm* available (and quite popular). The modification simply feeds the rc file through a filter, allowing us to preprocess the configuration details and to provide group-specific variants and easy user customization. Our scheme could have been implemented for *twm*, or indeed for any other window manager, by generating suitable configuration files as part of the session start-up, but there are a couple of small advantages to filtering:

- The purpose of the rc file, if any, in the user's home directory is the same as before, so that printed documentation and manual pages are less likely to cause confusion.

- You can change and immediately reload the configuration files without having to remember to regenerate an intermediate version first.

The default filter is a shell script wrapper that passes the *.twmrc* file through *cpp* along with some useful macro definitions. (A previous version of the filter used *m4* in place of *cpp*, but because users were much more familiar with the latter, we switched when we moved from X11R3 to X11R4.) This use of *cpp* does mean that # can no longer be used as a comment indicator, which is one of the few incompatibilities between our version and "standard" *twm*, but this has not caused users any major problems. In fact, the filter can also be substituted by the user, but few users actually do this.

We split the default rc file into several subfiles, which are #included into the main file. *cpp* is set up to search the following directories in order:

1. *HOME/lib/twm*
2. <LibDir>/*twm*/<group>
3. <LibDir>/*twm*

This allows course organizers to override the global defaults, with individual preferences taking priority over the others. The subfiles are arranged by logical function: one controls the host menus, one the mouse bindings, one the keypad bindings, and so on. In particular, different categories of users are presented with different host menus, listing only the hosts to which they have a legitimate reason to connect.

The default session script runs *twm* as the last, session-defining client, though this too is subject to user preference. If the environment variable XWM is defined in the user's *.x11rc* file, then this is used instead of *twm*. Normally this would point to another window manager, though it is sometimes useful to define it instead as the quit-button client or as an *xterm*.

DEFAULT CLIENTS

In contrast to resource definition and window manager configuration, the initial set of clients is taken completely from the user's own *.x11rc* file or from the group-specific file or from the global default file. There are a couple of reasons for this:

- Resources can be easily overridden when the user's preferences are merged, but it is easier not to start a client than it is to kill it once it has started (and perhaps to have to tidy up after it).

- In general, only a handful of clients are started, so there is no advantage in breaking down the configuration files into smaller functional units, in contrast to the window manager configuration, which is both quite complex and amenable to subdivision.

The actual mechanism by which this is implemented is simple: if there is an *.x11rc* file in the user's home directory, then use it; else if there is a group-specific file, then use that; else use the global default file.

A special "quit button" client, *xquitbutton*, is usually provided as part of these defaults, as this is a more obvious route to terminating the session than would be a window-manager menu option (though this is also provided) or a distinguished *xterm* client. A dialog box asks for confirmation; if it is given, the session-defining process is killed, returning the user to the "login" prompt or the *xdm* login or chooser window. Other default clients typically include an *xterm* or two, an editor, and a mail watcher.

SECURITY

In our department, with potentially mischievous or untrustworthy users and full Internet access for many of our systems, X security is of some concern. Our physical network topology is such that passive snooping on our ethers is generally not a problem, while breached password or file-system security would open up possibilities far beyond those available by attacking an X server. At the same time, a simple host-based mechanism would be insufficient, as this would not adequately protect X terminals served off multi-user machines.

We have therefore adopted the token-based mit-magic-cookie-1 authentication scheme. All of our workstations and most of our X terminals are secured in this way, with the cookie being generated either by *xdm* or in the shell-specific start-up script by a utility that seeds a random-number generator with some "hard-to-predict" values. Because home directories are automounted on all (departmental) systems, the cookie, once generated, is available to all clients no matter which system they are being run on.

One minor complication arises with *su*-like commands that change the user's real-user and effective-user IDs. Setuid utilities can either revert to their real user-ID[†] while extracting the cookie from the authorization file, or obtain access to system resources under their effective-user ID before reverting to their real-user ID to access the authorization file and open the display. This possibility, however, is no longer available to clients started after an *su*, as they have lost all information about their previous user ID. Our local *nsu* utility gets around this by extracting all the relevant cookies from the caller's authorization file under the caller's

---

† This is complicated somewhat by the semantics of the SysV `setuid()` system call when the effective-user ID is root.

real ID, saving them in memory, changing real and effective IDs, and finally storing the saved cookies into the authorization file corresponding to the new ID.

REMOTE CLIENTS

In addition to the host that users initially logged into, there are a number of other hosts available to most of our users. These include our department's own multiuser machines and compute-servers, as well as systems operated by the University's Computing Services and other departments and by outside bodies. Access to these may involve intermediate hosts, and since users are generally not interested in the means used to reach any particular host, we provide a shell script (*rterm*) to hide the details of the access mechanisms.

In fact, most users never call this script directly. Instead, it is usually invoked indirectly from a window manager menu. This is set up, often on a per-group basis though there is a system-wide default, so as to contain most of the hosts that the user is likely to want (or is likely to be authorized!) to connect to, and with the appropriate access-mechanism selection flags set.

The script usually invokes a local or remote *xterm* but can optionally run any other suitable client. The script does the following:

- It decides which machine is to host the *xterm* client, depending on whether that *xterm* is to provide an interactive shell or to run some other program such as *telnet, tip*, or *pad*.
- It constructs a suitable DISPLAY variable, depending on whether the *xterm* is to run on the same machine as the X server, on another machine in our local domain, or on a remote machine in another domain.
- It constructs an application instance name and a title for the window manager's title bar.
- It propagates the user's PATH and LD_LIBRARY_PATH, unless this is disabled by a command-line option.
- For alien hosts, it extracts and propagates the user's authorization cookie, or alternatively runs *xhost* + for the remote host, as directed by a command-line option.
- It runs the *xterm* client from a utility that redirects `stdout` and `stderr` to a log file, redirects `stdin` to */dev/null*, and closes all other possible file descriptors.

The purpose of closing or redirecting the *xterm* client's file descriptors is to dissociate it from any daemon that might have been required to invoke it. A program was found to be more reliable than any attempts to deal with the vagaries of the shell syntax and daemon options of various systems.

ANONYMOUS FTP

The paper and technical notes mentioned earlier are available by anonymous ftp from *ftp.dcs.ed.ac.uk* in the file *pub/lfu/doc.shar.Z*, with the automatic nightly update software in *pub/lfu/lfu.tar.Z*.

The components of the environment described in this paper can be obtained by anonymous ftp from the following:

- *ftp.dcs.ed.ac.uk*, in the file *pub/X11R5/dcs-environment.tar.Z*, or

- *export.lcs.mit.edu* and its usual shadows, in the file *contrib/edinburgh-environment.-tar.Z*.

This file contains our local clients and utilities, the *twm* patch, the scripts described here, copies of our *twm* and *xdm* configuration files, and our *site.def* installation configuration file.

CONCLUSIONS

Whether or not you consider our environment "large," it is certainly big enough that X system management is qualitatively different from that necessary at "small" sites or where users are mainly X literate. Although there may be one or two rough edges in the actual implementation, the underlying framework is sound and has proven to be extremely useful to our users, course organizers, and system support staff alike.

There are three main ways in which our environment succeeds:

- It makes installation on 20 (or even 200) fileservers as straightforward as on one.

- It is unobtrusive and is therefore less likely to be broken by careless or inexperienced users.

- It makes customization, where necessary, both flexible and easy.

Indeed, whether or not you choose to adopt any of the ideas described here, we would suggest that some kind of systematic treatment of configuration files is essential for any site with more than a fairly small number of competent users.

REFERENCES

Paul Anderson, "Managing program binaries in a heterogeneous UNIX network," *Proceedings of LISA V Conference*, USENIX, 1991, pp. 1–9.

Paul Anderson and Alastair Scobie, "The Local UNIX directory hierarchy," Technical note CS-TN-21, Department of Computer Science, University of Edinburgh, August 1991.

Paul Anderson, "Installing software on the Computer Science Department network," Technical note CS-TN-24, Department of Computer Science, University of Edinburgh, August 1991.

ACKNOWLEDGMENTS

Several of the support staff of our department contributed to the environment described here, in particular Paul Anderson, who wrote the original versions of many of the scripts. Helpful comments from our users also resulted in useful modifications and enhancements.

X APPLICATION DEBUGGING

Adrian Nye

ABSTRACT

This paper describes many of the techniques that experienced X programmers use to debug X code. It begins with standard debugging techniques and then describes techniques that deal specifically with the unique problems encountered in Xt and Xlib programming.

BASIC STRATEGIES

This section describes the basic techniques such as inserting printing commands, using source-level debuggers, using lint, and using debugging versions of libraries. It also mentions various commercial tools available. If all of these techniques and tools are familiar to you, feel free to skip this section. However, most programmers are not aware of all of them or do not use them in the most effective ways.

PRINTING DEBUGGING OUTPUT

It is a good idea to insert the equivalent of `printf` statements (controlled by symbols) in your code while writing the code. Some people say there is no need for `printf` because you can achieve the same result with a source-level debugger such as *dbx*. But there is a difference. First of all, you have to type in *dbx* commands every time you recompile the program and restart *dbx*, which gets tedious. Second, you know best what is supposed to be happening when you first write the code, so this can be the most efficient time to insert printing commands. If inserted so that they can be skipped using special compile-time options, these print statements can be left in place to aid in debugging after you have forgotten exactly how the code was supposed to operate. In other words, they are a form of comment as well as a debugging aid. Finally, debugging output throughout a program can help you catch errors you think are in one piece of code but are actually in code you are assuming to be bug-free. *dbx* and similar tools are great, but they don't completely replace the print statement.

One way to insert `printf`s is to do it between `#ifdef`/`#endif` pairs that check a symbol such as DEBUG, so that you can compile a version without the debugging code and not have to remove (and probably later reinsert) the debugging code. Here is an example:

```
#ifdef DEBUG
printf("main: current state is %s, %d\n", string, number);
#endif
```

You would compile the program to include these commands as follows:

```
% make "CDEBUGFLAGS = -DDEBUG -g"
```

This assumes you built the *Makefile* by using *imake*. If you didn't us *imake*, you'll need to edit the *Makefile* to pass `-DDEBUG` to the C compiler (which passes it to the preprocessor).

One caution: it is easy to be misled by `printf` if you forget to place a `\n` on the end of each one. Without `\n`, the output is buffered and may not appear when you expect it—or it may not appear at all (if the program dumps core). Another way to control buffering is with the `setbuf()` call.

The best way to insert debugging print commands is to use a macro that supports various debugging levels or codes. By allowing you to turn on or off different sets of debugging print statements, it lets you easily control how much printed output you see, guarantees the consistent use of \n, and differentiates debugging statements from public error reporting statements.[†]

Sam Black of Concurrent Computer Corporation has a similar setup in his *useful.h* file. If DEBUG is defined, the macros execute unconditionally. If cDEBUG is defined, their execution depends on the value of DBflag. If neither is defined, the macros produce no code. Here is an example:

```
DEB((stderr, "at point 1, a+b = %d\n", a+b));
DMSG(at point 2);
DPR(value, d);
DPA(array, index, d);
DBS(if (x < 0) EMSG(x is negative.));
```

It would produce something like this:

```
at point 1, a+b = 6
at point 2
value = 11
array[index] = 13;
In file main.c at line 16:  x is negative.
```

Note that PR, PS, PA, DPR, DMSG, and DPA depend on traditional style *cpp*, where you can do parameter substitution inside strings within a macro.

These macros can be easily modified to support debug levels instead of a simple debug flag. Here are his macros:

```
/*
**   Error macros
*/
#define _FL_              __FILE__, __LINE__
#define ERR(x)            fprintf(stderr, "In file %s at line %d:  ",
_FL_), \
                    fprintf x
#define EMSG(x)           fprintf(stderr, "In file %s at line %d:  %s\n",
_FL_, x)
#define cEMSG(eflag, x)      (eflag ? EMSG(x) : 0)
#define cERR(eflag, x)       (eflag ? ERR(x) : 0)
#define PERROR(x)            perror(x), exit(-1)


/*
**   Debug macros
*/
```

---

† Some UNIX utilities such as *uucp* have debugging output permanently compiled in and controlled by a command-line option.

```
#ifdef cDEBUG
#        ifdef MAIN
                char DBflag = FALSE;
#                undef MAIN
#        else
                extern char DBflag;
#        endif MAIN
#else
#        define DBflag 1
#endif cDEBUG

#if defined(DEBUG) || defined(cDEBUG)
#        define DEB(x)               (DBflag ? fprintf x : 0)
#        define DMSG(x)              (DBflag ? PS(x) : 0)
#        define DPR(x, f)            (DBflag ? PR(x, f) : 0)
#        define DPA(x, i, f)         (DBflag ? PA(x, i, f) : 0)
#        define DBS(s)               s
#else
#        define DEB(x)
#        define DMSG(x)
#        define DPR(x, f)
#        define DPA(x, i, f)
#        define DBS(s)
#endif defined(DEBUG) || defined(cDEBUG)

#define PS(x)                fprintf(stderr, "%s\n", x)
#define PR(x, f)          fprintf(stderr, "x = %f\n", x)
#define PA(x, i, f)          fprintf(stderr, "x[i] = %f\n", x[i])
```

USING LINT

It's a good idea to run lint on your code as soon as you can get it compiled or before you assume it to be bug-free. lint can catch some errors that the compiler misses, many of which waste memory or cause core dumps. Also, if there are any persistent compiler warnings, there is probably a bug that you haven't found yet.

The right way to invoke lint is to run it at once on all the source files that make up a program. Otherwise it can't check the consistency of references between files. If you use *imake* (and you should), one easy way to use lint is to invoke a lint target in the *Imakefile* by using the ComplexProgramTarget rule in your *Imakefile*. If you are using ComplexProgramTarget, you can put the following at the end of your *Imakefile*.[†]

```
LintTarget()
```

---

† All of this assumes you are using the X11 (or Motif) *imake* configuration files.

If you are a bit confused by *imake*, the book *Software Portability with imake*, recently published by O'Reilly & Associates, explains it all for you.

SOURCE-LEVEL DEBUGGING

If you do not have a source-level debugger such as *dbx*, you should get one. *gdb* is available free from the Free Software Foundation, but to use it you will also need to use their C compiler *gcc*. That's not a bad idea anyway, since *gcc* has an ANSI-C mode that can detect type errors, and it produces faster or more compact binaries than some commercial compilers. Recent versions of *gcc* and *gdb* also include C++ support.

Even if you think you know *dbx*, it is worthwhile rereading the manual page carefully. It has a lot of commands, and some of them can save time if you know they exist. Many programmers create a *.dbxinit* file to alias most of the common *dbx* commands to single letters:

```
alias c cont
alias p print
alias r run
alias t trace
alias s status
alias q quit
alias d delete
alias n next
alias sa "stop at"
```

A lot of people also don't know that *dbx* can handle complex macros with argument substitution. For example, if you are debugging widget code, you might want a macro like the following:

```
alias pwc "print ((WidgetRec*)(!:1))->core"
```

This can be used as follows

```
(dbx) pwc button1
```

With any source-level debugger, you should have another terminal from which you can log into your machine. Otherwise, if you set a break point that happens to be during a grab (which is easy to do), it can be difficult or impossible to regain control, and you will have to reboot. With the extra terminal, you can kill the debugger process when this happens.

To use a source-level debugger, your source must be compiled with the -g option. To get an *imake*-generated *Makefile* to build object files and executables that have symbol tables for the debugger, you can use CDEBUGFLAGS as shown earlier.

Some people use *sdb* to investigate core dumps and to help find mistakes like pointer errors. *sdb* has a rather obscure command syntax and output format, so it will take some practice to control it and interpret what it says.

DEBUGGING VERSIONS OF LIBRARIES

Many programmers find it helpful to have debugging versions of the X and Motif libraries, and instrumented memory-allocating libraries.

Since the X source code is available free and the Motif source code is available at a low cost, why not take advantage of this? For one thing, having debugging libraries allows you to use the source-level debugger more effectively, because it can show you the arguments passed to various library routines. It also becomes tempting to modify the Motif code so that it does what you think it should do. But this makes it difficult to patch the code to incorporate bug fixes, and you may need to redo this work every time a new release comes out.

Another thing to watch out for is the temptation to think that bugs are in the libraries rather than in your code. Most of the time they are in your code. Of course, if you do find a reproduceable bug, OSF and the X Consortium supply bug-report forms on which you can report it.

Various instrumented and debugging versions of `malloc` and `free` are available that help you track what memory is allocated and what is freed. They can also catch errors such as an attempt to free NULL pointers.

HELPFUL COMMERCIAL PRODUCTS

If you're developing a commercial product, you should consider purchasing one of three tools:

- Purify, from Pure Software (408-720-1600)
- CodeCenter, from CenterLine Software (800-922-3229 in the U.S.)
- Sentinel Debugging Environment, from Virtual Technologies (703-430-9247)

These tools seem expensive, but they can speed up programming and can help locate subtle problems such as memory leaks, which we will discuss further. These are only some of the leading tools.

One free integrated programming environment that can detect memory leaks is FIELD, by Steven Reiss from Brown University.

TESTING

Try multiple client systems, multiple X servers, and several window managers. You can get away with some surprising bugs on one system that will crash a program on another. For example, uninitialized variables may by luck have a valid value on one system but not on another.

There are products available that make it possible to test a GUI-driven product on multiple systems, even under different window systems, using the same script of user commands. See *THE X RESOURCE*, Issue 3, for a description of one of them.

X TOOLKIT AND MOTIF

Each library presents its own set of debugging challenges. This section describes some of the problems associated with Xt and Motif.

DESTROYING WIDGETS

Several problems can occur when you destroy widgets before the application exits:

- Many programs register callbacks, workprocs, or times with a widget as `client_data`. If the widget is destroyed and any of these functions are subsequently called, these functions will be passed a dangling pointer to a destroyed widget. One way to handle this is to unregister the function and then register it again with a valid widget as `client_-data`.

- One defensive programming trick is to insert debugging code that calls `XtIsObject()` to check the widget pointer at the beginning of every callback, timeout, or workproc function. It prints an explanatory message if an invalid pointer is passed.

- Another bug is calling `XtDestroyWidget` on a widget that has already been destroyed. This is allowed if the calls occur within one invocation of `XtDispatchEvent`, but it causes a core dump when the calls are in separate invocations.

- Some widgets do not free all the memory that they allocate. In addition, Xt does not free things like compiled translation tables. So there is always at least a small amount of memory leak when you create and delete widgets.

The resulting advice is this: don't create and destroy lots of widgets. A better approach is to reuse widgets by resetting their resources.

XTSETARG() VERSUS VARARG FUNCTIONS

Many Xt functions come in two varieties that differ in how you set resources. One requires an arglist set up using `XtSetArg()`, and the other specifies resources directly in a variable-length argument list (known as varargs).

Using `XtSetArg()` results in code that is hard to read and that is subject to bugs either because you forget to increment the counter each time you set an element in an argument list or because you exceed the allocated size of the arglist. To avoid forgetting to increment the counter, most programmers increment it on the same line. But this leads to a tricky bug related to `XtSetArg` that occurs when it is used within an if statement without brackets. This code looks like what you want, but it isn't:

```
if (boolean) /* wrong */
    XtSetArg(args[num_args], XtNheight, 100); num_args++;

XtSetValues(...);
```

In this code, `num_args` is always incremented regardless of the value of `boolean`. The defensive programming solution is to always put brackets around your if statements. This also makes it easier to add more code later to the if statements. An obvious work-around to this problem that leads to yet another subtle bug is this:

```
if (boolean)
    XtSetArg(args[num_args++], XtNheight, 100);
```

This one fails because the `XtSetArg()` macro refers to its first argument twice, so `num_args` is incremented twice.

Code using the varargs functions is much easier to read (and as we've seen, less error-prone) than code using `XtSetArg()`. Even if you eventually want to eliminate the varargs functions to remove their very slight performance penalty, it is wise to use them while debugging.

Many of Motif's convenience functions require the use of `XtSetArg()`, because there is no varargs equivalent (as of Motif 1.2). However, when the convenience function is creating a simple widget, you can use the varargs version of standard Xt routines instead. The convenience functions that create multiple widgets or that create specially configured widgets (like `XmCreateMenuBar()`) probably should be used as is.

CUSTOM WIDGETS

Debugging a custom widget is much easier if you use some tools. One tool is *editres*, which you use to test various resource settings. You simply create a simple test application with your widget and the Athena widgets (which have *editres* support built in). Then you run *editres* and the application and set resource by using the resource box.

Some interactive GUI builder programs can support custom widgets and are excellent for exercising all the resource settings. This is particularly good for a geometry-managing widget, since the widget can be interactively resized with children inside it.

MEMORY LEAKS

A memory leak happens when your application (or Xt or Motif) allocates memory but never frees it. It can result in your application eating up more and more memory the longer it runs.

As described earlier, one known area of memory leakage occurs when a widget is created and then destroyed. The best thing to do is to minimize the number of destroyed widgets. Instead, reuse them.

Compound strings also lead to memory leaks if not handled properly. The correct way to create a compound string in code and pass it to a function is the following:

```
/* value of variable "char * string" extracted from resource database */
XmString str = XmStringCreateLocalized(string);

widget = XtVaCreateManagedWidget("widget_name",
```

```
        xmPushButtonWidgetClass, parent,
    XmNlabelString, str,
    NULL);

    XmStringFree(str);
```

This code is incorrectly written as follows:

```
    widget = XtVaCreateManagedWidget("widget_name",
    xmPushButtonWidgetClass, parent,
    XmNlabelString, XmStringCreateLocalized(string),
    NULL);
```

The problem with the preceding code is that it creates a compound string, which allocates memory, but it does not save the pointer to this memory. So the memory can never be freed.

Another leak involves querying strings with XtGetValues() (or XtVaGetValues()). These functions usually return a pointer to a newly copied string, not to the widget's internal string. So this string must be freed once it is no longer needed. Otherwise, each call to XtGetValues() eats up more memory. Note that you must free the string before you call XtGetValues() for the same variable; otherwise, the original pointer is lost and there is no way to free the memory allocated by the previous XtGetValues(). Also note that you must use XmStringFree(), not XtFree(), because Motif Compound strings can have multiple elements and XtFree() will free only the first one.

If you are querying a Motif Compound string but need the string in char * form, you need to call XmStringGetLtoR() or an equivalent to extract the normal string from the compound string. XmStringGetLtoR() also copies the string, so you also have to free the memory it allocates. This time you should use XtFree().

Other than strings, most queried resources are read-only values and must not be freed. The exceptions are normally resources that are passed as pointers or IDs. Some of these exceptions are that you need to free the XFontStruct referenced in an XmFontList(), allocate and free the Shell widget's geometry resource, and allocate and free the XawList widget's list resource.

Many convenience functions return allocated memory that you must free. Most of the time you can tell these from a careful reading of the argument descriptions.

TYPE MISMATCHES

XmTextPosition (long) is not the same as Position (short). int is not the same as Dimension (an unsigned int). Be careful also when subtracting Dimensions and setting the result into another Dimension, since they are unsigned quantities.

Defensive programming: use a type-checking compiler such as C++ or ANSI-C. Or at least use lint.

LAYOUT PROBLEMS

It is sometimes difficult to get the layout you want. The first step is to use several levels of composite widgets so that each one has a fairly simple layout task. For example, if you have 100 widgets visible in your top-level window, group them by related function and put each set into a separate geometry-managing widget. Then put all these groups into a second level of geometry-managing widget. You can also put one or more composite widgets plus some simple widgets into another composite widget.

Unfortunately, using multiple composite widgets often leads to nonintuitive behavior of Motif tab groups. The user should not be expected to understand how the geometry-managing widgets are nested. So you may need to do some manual manipulation of the tab order.

If you set resources for composite or constraint widgets incorrectly, it is possible for some widgets to overlap, and therefore some can be hidden. *editres* (especially its flash feature) is useful for finding missing widgets. It tells you whether they are hidden or unmapped, perhaps because you never managed them.

XLIB AND X PROTOCOL

Here are several of the areas of Xlib programming that catch beginners.

PIXMAPS

Unlike Windows, Pixmaps have undefined contents when they are first created. So, on some architectures, if you create a pixmap and then copy it directly to a window, the window may contain random garbage. If you need a pixmap with a known value in every pixel, you must draw that value into every pixel. The easiest way to do this is with `XFillRectangle()`.

If you create very large pixmaps, you should be prepared for BadAlloc errors. The server may run out of memory or it may have an arbitrary maximum pixmap size, like the size of the screen.

BOUNDARY CONDITIONS

Because `Position` is defined as a 16-bit signed integer, and `Dimension` is defined as a 16-bit unsigned integer, it is possible to create a window four times larger (in area) than the area you can actually draw into or receive input events from. To avoid the problems related to windows that are too big, make sure that windows and pixmaps are no bigger that 32,767 pixels square. This size can be reached in applications where a large window is viewed through a viewport, particularly in text editors or viewers where opening huge files or changing to large font sizes can create huge documents.

Each server defines a maximum request size of at least 16k bytes. This size can be reached in the drawing functions `XDrawLines()`, `XDrawArcs()`, `XFillPolygon()`, some text drawing routines, and in R4 also in several other functions. Your program should calculate the maximum number of elements it can draw in one call, by using `XMaxRequestSize()`. The maximums are shown in Table 1.

FUNCTION	MAXIMUM NUMBER OF ELEMENTS
`XDrawPoint`[a]	`(XMaxRequestSize(dpy) - 3)` points
`XFillPolygon`	`(XMaxRequestSize(dpy) - 4)` points
`XDrawRectangles`[a], `XFillRectangles`[a]	`((XMaxRequestSize(dpy) - 3) / 2)` rectangles
`XDrawSegments`[a], `XDrawLines`	`((XMaxRequestSize(dpy) - 3) / 2)` lines or segments
`XDrawArcs, XFillArcs`[a]	`((XMaxRequestSize(dpy) - 3) / 3)` arcs

TABLE 1: *THE MAXIMUM NUMBER OF ELEMENTS FOR EACH DRAWING FUNCTION*

a. Limit applies only for R4 and earlier versions of Xlib.

For text-drawing routines, the maximum size depends on the number and length of the strings.

X PROTOCOL ERRORS

You know you have an X Protocol error when a program quits unexpectedly and you see a message like this:

```
X Error of failed request: BadWindow (invalid Window parameter)
Major opcode of failed request: 2 (X_ChangeWindowAttributes)
Resource id in failed request: 0x0
Serial number of failed request: 16
Current serial number in output stream: 17
```

The first step in debugging X protocol errors is synchronization.

In Xlib programs, turn on synchronous mode in a debugger by setting _Xdebug to 1 before `XOpenDisplay()` is called:

```
(dbx) assign _Xdebug = 1
(dbx) run
X Error of failed request: BadWindow (invalid Window parameter)
...
```

In Xt programs, run the program with the `-synchronous` command-line option (which can be abbreviated):

```
(dbx) run -sync
X Error of failed request: BadWindow (invalid Window parameter)
...
```

Then find out where the program died:

```
(dbx) where
exit (0x1) at 0x331be
_XDefaultError(0x41000, 0x7fffd900) at 0x76e9
_XError(0x41000, 0x7fffd9bc) at 0x778b
_XReply(0x41000, 0x7fffd9bc, 0x7, 0x0) at 0x68bb
_XQueryFont(0x41000, 0x500004, 0x7fffda44) at 0x2519
XLoadQueryFont(0x41000, 0x3423e) at 0x2519
load_font(font_info = 0x7fffda70), line 255 in "basicwin.c"
main(argc = 2, argv = 0x7fffdb6c, 0x7fffdb78), line 155 in "basicwin.c"
```

Surprisingly, XLoadQueryFont() is not the source of the error. Note that in the error report the current serial number is 17 while the failed-request serial number is 16. So we should look for the error in the command immediately before XLoadQueryFont(). In this case the command was XSelectInput(), which actually generates a ChangeWindowAt-tributes() protocol request (this clue was also in the error report).

Some programmers report that their versions of *dbx* identify the exact call containing the error, even when the serial number of the error is different from the current serial number. In either case, you can locate the problem within a line or two—which is close enough.

Here are some of the more common but subtle bugs that cause protocol errors:

- BadMatch errors: Depth mismatches. GCs have a depth; they can be used only to draw into windows and pixmaps of the same depth. A GC's depth is specified by passing a window when creating the GC. In Xt the GC depth is the same as the widget (or the nearest windowed ancestor for a gadget) passed to XtGetGC(). Normally, all widgets have the screen's default depth unless you specified otherwise.Often this error appears only on color screens, since on monochrome screens all useful pixmaps have depth 1.

- Look for "Window in failed request 0x0," where Window can also be any other resource such as Pixmap or Colormap. This means that you passed in a resource that hasn't been created yet, or somehow you don't have the right value in the variable you passed. If a number looks valid, then perhaps you already destroyed that resource. If you are programming in Xt and want to know which widget uses the window mentioned in the error, you can type the following:

```
(dbx) print XtWindowToWidget(dpy, windowid)
```

- If you can't see immediately what's wrong with the function call, check your Xlib documentation (or X Protocol documentation) to see what causes X protocol errors for this function. Also, look up the list of errors, since this describes what kind of mistakes generates each type of error. If you want to use the X Protocol documentation, you'll need a table that maps each Xlib function into the X Protocol request it uses. Such a table is included in O'Reilly Volume Zero, *X Protocol Reference Manual*.

Note that some X protocol errors can occur as a result of problems unrelated to programmer error. For example, BadAlloc can happen when the X server runs out of memory, which is more common on PC X servers and X terminals. So, most applications should define their own X protocol error handlers to provide messages explaining what went wrong and what to do, instead of just the normal X protocol error report.

REGISTERING YOUR OWN ERROR HANDLER

Xlib has two types of error handlers: one for fatal errors such as a broken connection with the X server, and one for nonfatal errors such as protocol errors.

There is no way to continue an application that succumbs to a fatal error, so the default handler reports the situation and exits. However, your application might want to save its data before exiting. If so, you will register a new fatal-error handler. But you can't use the X server to ask the user anything, since no more requests to the X server can be made. So this has to be automatic without user input.

The nonfatal-error handler handles many of the routine errors such as BadWindow. Most of these indicate programmer error, and you have hopefully eliminated them by the time the application reaches users. But the user can still get BadAlloc errors. So most programs should register a new handler that is the same as the default handler for most errors but substitutes a more explanatory message for BadAlloc errors (and perhaps saves application data). For example, it might say (in an *xterm*) "The server doesn't have sufficient memory for the requested operation. Please quit some applications and try again." It is supposed to be possible to continue running the application, although I haven't actually tried it or seen it done.

X PROTOCOL SNOOPING

Sometimes to debug a problem you need to see the actual protocol requests and events as they pass between the server and the client. All the protocol viewers interpose a pseudoserver process, which acts like a server to the client and acts like a client to the real X server. If you are on a workstation with one X, which you connect to as hostname:0, you would connect to the pseudoserver by specifying hostname:1.

The oldest and best-known protocol viewer is *xscope*. Its weakness is that it shows you everything that passes between the server and the client. A good alternative is *xmonui* and *xmond*, a pair of programs that work together. *xmond* is a daemon that monitors all the traffic between the client and the server, and *xmonui* is a GUI program that allows you to control what types of information you want to see. These programs are available on *export.lcs.mit.edu*.

Network General sells a commercial protocol sniffer that reputedly is good for really low-level protocol analysis. It handles not only X but things like NFS or even raw TCP/IP.

EXPERIENCES IN EXTENDING X TO PROVIDE DETERMINISM

Robert Chesler

ABSTRACT

With the advent of the POSIX.4 standard, the increasing speed of hardware, and the efforts of companies like Concurrent Computer Corporation who serve the market demand for real-time open systems, an increasing number of real-time applications can be addressed with UNIX-based distributed computing solutions. The X Window System is the natural graphics software system for these applications because of its network-based client/server architecture, platform independence, thousands of software applications, and graphical user interface (GUI) toolkits and widget sets such as Motif™.

However, many real-time applications require not only a real-time operating system but also a real-time graphics system that provides the "three Ps" of real-time: priority, preemption, and predictability. Standard X does not address these requirements. But since X is extensible, it was possible to implement an extension to the X protocol that does address these issues.

Members of Concurrent's graphics and operating systems development groups designed the cccRealTime extension to X. As a member of the graphics group, I worked to help implement this extension, which Concurrent now offers as a product called RealTimeX. In this article I describe the obstacles to achieving determinism in X and how we overcame them.

Robert Chesler is an independent software consultant specializing in the X Window System and the UNIX operating system. In his prior work at Concurrent Corporation, he applied UNIX systems to the real-time tasks of computer music and centrifugal earthquake modelling. Mr. Chesler is also known for his work in developing the XTrap extension to X protocol. He holds a BSE in electrical engineering and computer science from Princeton University.

REAL-TIME SHORTCOMINGS OF STANDARD X

A real-time system is one in which the correctness of the computation depends not only on the correctness of the computation but also on the time at which the result is produced. If the timing constraints of the system are not met, system failure is said to have occurred. Hence, it is essential that the timing constraints of the system are guaranteed to be met. Thus, real-time can range from the processing of high-frequency satellite data to a weekly payroll system, both of which are as time critical as they are accuracy critical.

The X server typically has many clients competing for a few resources, such as the frame buffer, graphics processor, input devices, and screen. Standard X deals out these resources in a consistent, "fair" fashion, treating all clients the same, just as standard time-sharing UNIX treats all processes the same. Likewise, windows are stacked in a consistent fashion that assumes that all windows are equally important. These policies do not take into consideration the fact that in real-time applications some clients are more important than others and some windows are more important to keep visible to the user than others. The key requirements for RealTimeX were to provide prioritization and preemption of clients, prioritization of windows, and means for X clients to be notified when their real-time constraints are not being met.

The unpredictability of X operations is due mainly to the nondeterminism of user activity and the nondeterminism inherent in distributed computing environments. Because X is designed to give the user control over the system, the programmer can't know or control when the X server will execute a request or when the results of the request will become visible. Distributed applications are likely to run on systems of widely varying hardware performance, and their degree of determinism is limited by latencies at several stages, as shown in Figure 1.

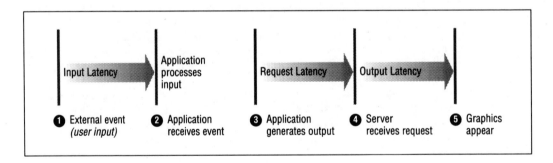

FIGURE 1: *LATENCIES LIMITING GRAPHICS DETERMINISM*

X increases the request latency by introducing the double function-call latency of Xlib and the GUI.

Predictability in terms of absolute guaranteed response time was not one of our goals, because many of these latencies are variable and are outside the control of the graphics software system. But we did provide mechanisms (markers, described later in this paper) by which client programs can monitor, measure, and adjust to server response, in order to ensure timely and correct output to the user. We employed markers in sample clients that show developers and users how well the system is responding.

Another non-goal was faster overall response. We provided faster response only in the sense that a particular client need not wait for other clients. Not surprisingly, however, it happens that applications can *seem* to respond faster when written with RealTimeX, because clients responsible for the display events in which the user is most interested can now use a higher priority than other clients, and unimportant clients can be given decreased priorities.

A PRIORITY-BASED SCHEDULER FOR CLIENTS

Standard X provides a simple round-robin scheduler. When a client establishes a connection with the server, it gets placed in a queue. All clients are treated equally. In real-time applications, however, some clients are more important than others, and the relative importance of clients can change dynamically.

To address this issue, we devised a priority-based scheduler that handles a high-priority client's requests before those of clients with lower priorities. In our priority-based scheduler, there are multiple queues, one for each priority level, as shown in Figure 2. Each client with requests goes on the queue reserved for that client's priority, where they are handled in a round-robin fashion. The server takes requests from the highest-priority queue first. Requests at lower priorities have to wait until all requests from clients with higher priorities have been handled.

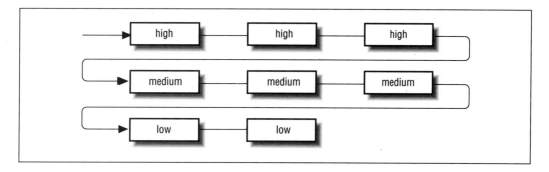

FIGURE 2: *REALTIMEX CLIENTS IN PRIORITIZED CLIENT QUEUES*

In standard X, only one client can grab the server. Under RealTimeX, a high-priority client is impervious to a lower-priority client's grab, and grabs are nested when a high-priority client grabs the server after the server has already been grabbed by one or more lower priority clients. Because grabs are nested, multiple clients at different priority levels can have the server grabbed at the same time.

We thus changed the semantics of the `XGrabServer()` request under RealTimeX so that clients at less than or equal to the grabbing client's priority are prevented from getting serviced by the X server.

The window manager normally uses a grab when rubber banding a box or when issuing a copy-area request to facilitate a window move. Under RealTimeX, if a large *xclock* with a one-second update on the second hand has been given the highest priority, for example, it will get the server's attention even when another client is rubber banding or when the window manager is moving a window.

There may be some incomplete draws, but the second hand will "keep on ticking," updating its second hand at one-second intervals without interruption. Instead of an *xclock*, of course, the high-priority client in a real-world, real-time application might be displaying a power-plant pressure gauge, an iconic "blip" on a digital radar display, or an aircraft image on a collision course in a flight simulator.

We found that it was reasonable in all cases to let the server handle user input at a higher priority than that of client requests. User input events are more important than even the highest-priority client, and the amount of time the server spends tracking user input is negligible. User input doesn't introduce latencies that are likely to be a problem for a real-time X client.

To provide backward compatibility, client priorities default to priority zero. In this case, all clients are at the same priority level, causing the priority-based scheduler to revert to one round-robin queue and only one grab allowed at a time.

TIME-BASED SCHEDULING VERSUS REQUEST-BASED SCHEDULING

For real-time applications, we felt that request-based scheduling was inadequate because of the vast differences in real processing time for various requests. For example, it is not reasonable to treat a `Sync` request the same as a full-screen `GetImage()` request in terms of processing time.

The standard X scheduler simply counts requests and accepts up to 10 requests from each client sharing the X server before proceeding to the next client. While this policy does share the X server's resources among multiple clients, it makes no provision for the varying amounts of time required for different requests, and therefore doesn't share these resources "fairly."

Under RealTimeX, scheduling can be time-based as well as request-based. The scheduler counts the amount of real time (not CPU time) spent by the server on each request. For example, the server can be configured to switch between clients every 40 milliseconds. The 40 milliseconds are called the *timeslice*. Under RealTimeX, a program can dynamically change the server's timeslice parameter. In a real application in which multiple clients are at the same priority level and a client repeatedly draws a complex update, such as an animation frame, there might be a natural timeslice parameter that results in the smoothest display, so the client can update its complex display in one shot, without interruption.

PREEMPTION GRANULARITY

We looked at fine-grain and coarse-grain preemption of requests by higher-priority requests. Coarse-grain preemption preserves the standard X notion of requests being atomic. In this model, once the server starts processing a single request, it does not stop. Thus, a `PutImage()` or a `GetImage()` request need not lock the window whose image it is dealing with.

But on slow-to-medium-performance host-based X servers, the processing latency for some requests can be significant compared with the request slice. So, we considered breaking the atomicity constraint and letting preemption occur at a finer grain. In the fine-grain preemption model, the X server could, in the middle of a request, save its state and start another request, either because a high-priority client issued a request or because the current timeslice has expired.

As our reference platform matured to a dedicated graphics processor, Concurrent's GA5000, we discovered that the extra effort of making the X server multithreaded and saving complicated states deep within DDX levels just wasn't worth the minor savings in latency, at least for the first released version of RealTimeX.

Thus, although the RealTimeX protocol provides a mechanism to describe fine-grain preemption, in a very high performance X server it is likely that standard X atomic behavior can be preserved without preventing a real-time X client from meeting its constraints.

MARKERS

To enhance the predictability of the X Window System, RealTimeX offers a method of using markers by which a client can adapt to the dynamic graphics performance of the X server. *Markers* are dummy requests that logically subdivide the client's stream of requests. They are like milestones, or delimiters around groups of requests.

The X client puts a marker onto the request stream, and the server sends back an event when it processes the request. Markers bear identifying numbers that increment with each call. The programmer can build synchronization and scheduling models on top of these simple calls.

With markers, an application can determine if there are too many outstanding graphics requests waiting for the X server to process. When there are too many requests in the queue, there is a significant latency before the user sees the graphics output. This is a "soft" real-time error.

A real-time application may need to detect the presence of soft real-time errors in the graphics subsystem and may need to respond automatically in an intelligent fashion. To adapt to this kind of error condition, a client can refine its graphics output. For example, an X client can decrease the detail in its graphics so that fewer X server resources are used to present the display, as shown in Figure 3.

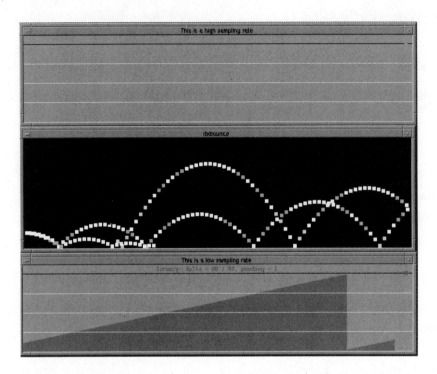

FIGURE 3: *A Demonstration of Adaptive Refinement Using Markers*

The strip chart at the top of the set of windows shown in Figure 3 displays a sawtooth wave form. The strip chart at the bottom, driven by a separate client at the same priority, displays a similar sawtooth wave form of a lower frequency. A third client is running in the window between the two strip charts, putting a periodic "bursty" load on the server. This client has a higher priority than the strip charts have, but the real-world constraints require that each strip-chart display be kept up to date, each displaying a vertical line corresponding to the latest acquired sample. During the peak load burst, the server is able to keep up with the demands of the lower-frequency strip chart, but it cannot keep up with the demands of the higher-frequency strip chart.

The strip-chart clients use RealTimeX markers to notice, by the number of outstanding markers, when the X server is failing to keep up. The high-frequency strip chart adapts its sampling rate during bursty periods and skips samples, decreasing its detail. By keeping its ordinate axis proportional with time, the proper data is still conveyed to the user. The dark regions in the graph indicate where samples are skipped.

EXPERIENCES IN EXTENDING X TO PROVIDE DETERMINISM

Without this adaptive refinement, the display would not keep up, and the user would get a stale view of the data. The application would be failing to meet its real-time constraint. In fact, in standard X, except for the fact that memory buffers are limited, there could be an almost unlimited amount of graphical data queued up that the user might see only when it is too late, or that might scroll off the screen too fast for the user to recognize.

A heart-rate monitor might use this kind of adaptive refinement. It might be important to judge, at a glance, the current regularity or irregularity of the patient's heartbeat. High-frequency components of the heartbeat might not be critical to conveying this information, so skipping samples while maintaining temporal accuracy would be a reasonable way to respond to server overload.

URGENT COMMUNICATIONS

If a client (such as the plaid demo) that can hog an X server is currently at a higher priority than that of an important client, the important client ought to have a way to request that the X server increase its own priority. If the request were part of the regular request stream, the server would not immediately process it. We needed to provide a way to make such a request in an urgent fashion so that it would be processed before any request in any client's regular request stream. We provided an "urgent channel" by which a RealTimeX client can send the server an urgent request to raise its priority, so that it can be scheduled ahead of other clients that currently have higher priorities. This feature enables developers to write clients that are "nice" as long as there is enough time for them to run, but they can assert themselves so that they are served in time when necessary. To ensure that no one client can hog the X server at an urgent priority, RealTimeX allows only certain kinds of requests to be made through the urgent channel.

CHANGING THE SEMANTICS OF WINDOW CIRCULATION

A principal goal of our efforts was to enable a programmer to guarantee the visibility of important windows. We implemented this by providing a scheme for window prioritization. Implementing window prioritization in X required developing new semantics for window circulation, in the standard X request `CirculateSubwindows`, such that a single circulation request triggers a "mini-circulation" in each priority level. Each window has a priority attribute, and the X server circulates all windows at a given priority level for each priority level that is present.

This scheme provides backward compatibility, preserving the behavior of standard X when all windows are at the default priority of 0 set by RealTimeX. It also preserves the standard intent to display every window through repeated circulations.

Window prioritization influences stacking order, and in this respect it takes some control away from the user and gives it to the programmer, for the sake of guaranteeing visibility of critical information.

We felt it would be useful, however, to give the user the opportunity to set initial window priorities through the X resource database. Every display has a cutoff priority that the user can set by means of an X resource. If there is a window with a higher priority than the cutoff priority, the X server disables the screen saver, and the window manager will not let the user move the window offscreen or iconify it. If the window is already offscreen or iconified, the window manager tries to move it back onscreen or deiconifies it.

We extended *mwm* (the Motif window manager) so that it would understand the internal state of the X server, with prioritized windows. Also, the window manager has to understand the cutoff priority semantics, since only the window manager controls window positioning and iconification.

In addition, with the window manager running, priority-change requests are intercepted by the window manager in the standard X way, since the window manager frame and decoration windows go between the client's top-level window and the X server's root window.

We developed tools to allow the user to control all the various real-time parameters of the RealTimeX environment, such as the priority attributes of all clients and windows and the tunable scheduler parameters. The priority management tools, *rtxwm* and *rtxpm*, provide a Motif GUI with sliders and scrollbars to interactively adjust priorities. A noninteractive utility, *rtxprio*, adjusts priority attributes by means of command-line options.

CONCLUSION

There is still much to learn from those who have added determinism to time-sharing operating systems. Their experiences will help us provide a complete deterministic graphics environment. But RealTimeX works today, and it allows real-time application developers to utilize the various benefits of the X window system without losing all the benefits of the real-time operating system upon which the X window system may be layered.

A TALE OF TWO TOOLKITS:

XT VERSUS INTERVIEWS

Imran Bashir and David M Sternlicht

ABSTRACT

This paper takes an objective look at developing an application by using the Intrinsics-based Athena widgets and the C++-based InterViews toolkit. The test application chosen is a color editor that interprets and sets stimuli values by using the X color management system (Xcms). A view-data paradigm was chosen to organize the relationship between the color displayed and its representation in the various color spaces.

Imran Bashir (ibashir@cat.syr.edu) co-authored this paper during a summer internship at the X Consortium. He can be reached at the Department of Electrical & Computer Engineering, 111 Link Hall, Syracuse University, Syracuse, NY 13244, where he is a doctoral student. Mr. Bashir holds a bachelor's degree in electrical engineering from UET, Lahore, Pakistan, and a master's degree in computer engineering from Syracuse University. His research interests include software engineering, software tools, object-oriented software, and testing of object-oriented software.

David M Sternlicht (dave@expo.lcs.mit.edu) is a former staff member of the X Consortium. He completed a master's degree in computer science at the University of Oregon in1980. He has worked for Hewlett Packard, General Electric, and MIT. On June 1, 1993, he began working at Automatix, a robotics company located in Billerica, MA.

INTRODUCTION

While they are orthogonal mechanisms, the use of color and the use of GUI toolkits are important tools through which modern programmers design their applications. Xcms, distributed with Release 5 of X11, has provided programmers with a more generic way of specifying colors and guaranteeing their consistency across different display terminals.

InterViews, soon to be called Fresco, has provided a new, and perhaps a more powerful and flexible, means of designing and implementing a user interface. InterViews is an object-oriented software system for window-based applications. It is a C++ interface to X windows, and it is built on top of X. It was implemented at Stanford University by Mark Linton's group. The name *InterViews* comes from the idea of a user interface object presenting an Interactive View of the same data [2]. InterViews provides a number of high-level components for building interfaces.

At present, only the 3.1Beta version of InterViews is available, with the promise of a complete 3.1 version sometime in the near future. Obviously, this version is not stable yet.

We have blended these two important systems to create a tool called *ice*, an InterViews-based color editor. *ice* represents the eight Xcms color spaces. Each color space is represented by a set of scrollbars, one per dimension of the color space. The value of each dimension is individually changeable. The effect of a change in a dimensions value for a color space is reflected in the dimensions of the other color spaces. Each color space is itself selectable in that it updates its values with a change in a value in some other color space. There is also a color-viewing area that displays the color for the given values of RGB on a display. At any point in time, the values of all color spaces are equivalent and correspond to the color that is displayed on the screen.

For an introduction to Xcms and the various color spaces, see "A Technical Introduction to the X Window System" by Al Tabayoyon, which appeared in Issue 0 of THE X RESOURCE.

GOALS

The main goal of this project was to build an application by using the InterViews toolkit. This would help determine the leverage InterViews can provide in building an application. The application that we chose is a multispace color editor. The two other intended benefits of this work were these:

- A color editor that represents all of the eight color spaces
- A comparison of InterViews with the Athena widgets

CONSTRAINTS

The following requirements and constraints were placed on the design in order to enhance the tool's usability:

- The tool should represent all the eight Xcms color spaces—RGB, RGBi, CIEXYZ, CIExyY, CIEu'v'Y, CIEL*u*v*, CIELab, and TekHVC.

- The value of any dimension in each of the preceding color spaces should be individually changeable.

- A change in one dimension of a color space should be reflected in all the other color spaces. Thus, a change in the value of H in TekHVC color space should update the values of all the dimensions in the other color spaces.

- There should be a color-viewing area that represents the color on that CRT for the current values of all color spaces.

- A user should be allowed to enable or disable any color space that he or she is interested in.

- The design of the tool should make it easy to add a new color space. In other words, the design should be enunciable.

This paper is organized as follows. The next section explains the design of the ColorEditor tool using InterViews, called *ice* hereafter. A second design, using the Athena widgets, is also given. The problems encountered during the design of this tool, especially in using InterViews and Xlib, are detailed in the following section. This is followed by a comparison of designs using InterViews and Athena widgets. The paper concludes with a discussion of what we have learned from the design of this tool. Some recommendations for InterViews are also given.

THE IMPLEMENTATION OF ICE

The following sections describe the implementation of *ice*, first by using InterViews and then by using the Athena widgets.

IMPLEMENTATION USING INTERVIEWS

The design of the *ice* tool has been driven primarily by the philosophy of data versus views. This dichotomy has a long history in the user interface community. Smalltalk divided information display into a Model-View-Controller triad [15]. In the Andrew toolkit, some of the most basic components are data objects and views [16]. InterViews follows in this tradition by also promoting the concept of different views of the same data.

The mechanism for supporting this in InterViews consists of three protocols: Adjustable, Observable, and Observer [2]. *Adjustables* handle requests to modify a viewing area in ways such as scrolling, paging, and zooming. An *Observable* takes care of a single dimension of an Adjustable and represents the InterViews notion of data. Observables communicate with a number of views, known as *Observers* in the InterViews toolkit. This is done through a notify-update protocol.

We have used these classes in designing our color editor. The hierarchy of classes is shown in Figure 1, and the design of the tool is shown in Figure 2.

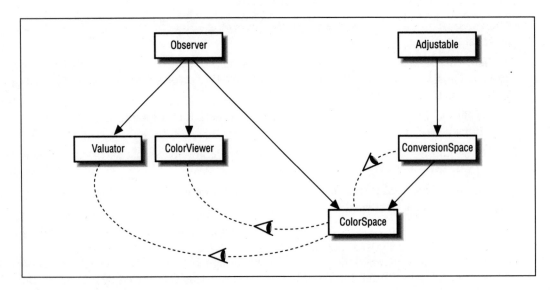

FIGURE 1: *THE HIERARCHY OF CLASSES, SHOWING THE OBSERVER–OBSERVABLE RELATIONSHIP*

The hierarchy figure indicates that ConversionSpace is an Adjustable while the ColorSpace is an Adjustable as well as an Observer. As an Observer, a ColorSpace observes a ConversionSpace. Through the Observables maintained by being an Adjustable, the ColorSpace lets both the ColorViewer and the Valuator objects observe itself. ColorViewer is an Observer and is responsible for updating the color-viewing area on the screen. One Valuator per dimension of a ColorSpace keeps a FieldEditor up to date and also lets a user change the value of that dimension through the FieldEditor.

In our design, ConversionSpace serves as common data while the ColorSpace objects act as several views of this data. Each ColorSpace uses the ConversionSpace object to convert between its local values (view) and the global values (common data). Every ColorSpace has three scrollbars to visually represent each color dimension. Three FieldEditors (subclassed from InputHandler) per ColorSpace textually show the values in each dimension of a Color-Space. Therefore, a value in a particular dimension can be changed either by moving the thumb of the corresponding scrollbar or by entering a number in the FieldEditor through the keyboard.

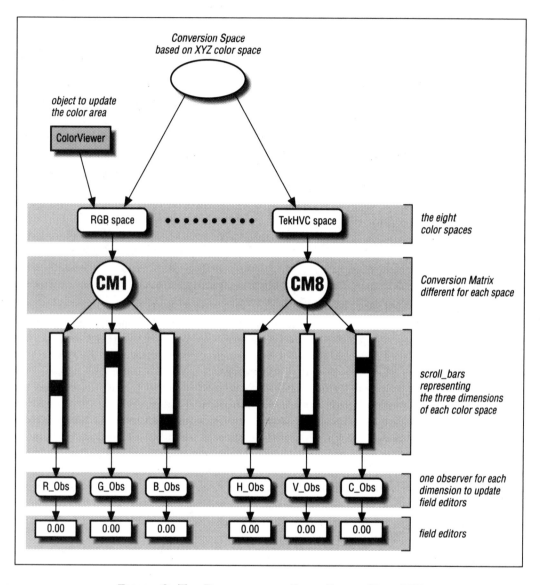

FIGURE 2: *THE DESIGN OF THE COLOREDITOR TOOL ICE*

The ColorViewer object is responsible for displaying the color and is therefore an Observer of the RGB ColorSpace. When there is a change in the values of this ColorSpace, the Color-Viewer is notified and it updates the ColorViewer's viewing area on the screen.

The dynamic execution of the *ice* program proceeds as follows:

1. Initialization: When a ConversionSpace is created, the values in the three dimensions of the ConversionSpace are each set to 0.5. When a ColorSpace is created, it calculates its local values by observing the ConversionSpace's values of X, Y, and Z, and then updates itself.

2. Manipulation: When a user changes a value in a ColorSpace, either by disturbing the position of a scrollbar or through a field editor, the following takes place:

   - A change in value calls the ColorSpace's `scroll_to` method. This method changes local color values to new values and then calls the routine `convert-ToXYZ()`, which changes XYZ values in the ConversionSpace object.

   - All the ColorSpaces are observers of the ConversionSpace object. As soon as a change is observed, a ColorSpace's update method is invoked.

   - `ColorSpace::update` calculates its local values by looking at the new values of X, Y, and Z in the ConversionSpace. Once the new values have been determined, local copies are updated.

   - This setting of local values also notifies any other Observers, namely Valuators or the ColorViewer, of this ColorSpace object.

A potential problem here is the possibility of an infinite loop. Consider the following scenario. A ColorSpace object, CS1, has a change in the value of one of its dimensions. This change in CS1 will also alter the values of the ConversionSpace object. A change in ConversionSpace alerts all its Observers to update themselves. Since CS1 is also an Observer of the ConversionSpace object, it will try to update itself without realizing that it was the one that had changed the ConversionSpace object to begin with. A simple Boolean data member `iSetConversionflag` is added to ColorSpace to indicate that an object is the initiator of a color change and that its values do not have to be updated with the change of X, Y, and Z in the ConversionSpace object.

IMPLEMENTATION USING XAW

The Athena widget implementation seeks to provide the extensibility provided by the Observable-Observer paradigm supported in InterViews. The latter implementation uses a single Observable to maintain a color data state, and various Observers to provide a view of this data. The Xaw implementation subclasses a color management object (CMSObject) from the Object class (a superclass of Core). This object provides resources as follows:

- An Xcms structure containing CIEXYZ data. This is our "data."

- A list of callbacks in which each callback performs a translation to a given color space. This is our set of "views."

Every set of color-space controls can be activated or deactivated by a toggle switch that adds or removes a callback from the CMSObject callback list. The design is extensible because, in order to add a conversion to another color space, one needs simply to add a callback to the list.

PROBLEMS ENCOUNTERED

This section describes some problems encountered during each implementation, and the chosen solutions.

INTERVIEWS

The major problem encountered with InterViews 3.1 was the handling of multiple dimensions. Let's first describe the problem in detail.

THE PROBLEM

The previous section described the three data-view protocols: Observable, Observer, and Adjustable. The declaration of dimensions in `iv/src/include/InterViews/geometry.h` looks like this:

```
typedef unsigned int DimensionName;

enum{
    Dimension_X = 0, Dimension_Y, Dimension_Z, Dimension_Undefined
};

class CoordinateSpace {
public:
    enum { x = 0, y, z, dimensions };
};
```

In the preceding standalone enum, four types of dimensions have been defined: `Dimension_X`, `Dimension_Y`, `Dimension_Z`, and `Dimension_Undefined`. This approach has two problems. One problem is with the Adjustable class itself, and the other problem is the representation of these dimensions through the `WidgetKit` class interface. Let's look at both of these problems individually.

The Adjustable Problem
An Adjustable object should be able to handle any number of dimensions. In an application in which a user has a three-dimensional space, an Adjustable object can be used as such. Each dimension in the application's 3-D space can be represented by the dimensions in the preceding standalone enum.

Assume that we have an n-dimensional space, where n = 4. We create a subclass of the Adjustable base class and call it FDAdjustable (for Four-Dimensional-Adjustable). We can declare the following to have the fourth dimension for this declared class:

```
enum { Dimension_W = 5}; // including Dimension_Undefined

class FDAdjustable : public Adjustable {
...
```

In this subclass we store all the information about the Dimension_W, such as the current value in the Dimension_W, and so on. Now if we create an object of the type FDAdjustable and try to attach an Observer to the Dimension_W, we create a serious programming error.[†] To comprehend why this happens, let's look at the constructor of our base class Adjustable.

```
struct AdjustableImpl {
private:
    friend class Adjustable;

    AdjustableInfo info_[CoordinateSpace::dimensions];
};

Adjustable::Adjustable() {
    impl_ = new AdjustableImpl;
    AdjustableImpl& a = *impl_;
    for (DimensionName d = 0; d < CoordinateSpace::dimensions;
            d++) {
        AdjustableInfo& i = a.info_[d];
        i.observable_ = new Observable;
        i.small_ = 1;
        i.large_ = 0;
    }
}
```

As we saw in the first code fragment of this chapter, the value of CoordinateSpace::dimensions is 3, and the index of AdjustableInfo info_ ranges from 0 to 2. Therefore, following a natural design impulse to add dimensions is bound to create problems.

In conclusion, one can only have three dimensions in an Adjustable, and any space with four or more dimensions has to be represented by more than one Adjustable.

The WidgetKit Class Problem

We have seen how the Adjustable class fails to handle more than three dimensions. Let's now turn our attention to representing these dimensions in the real world.

---

† Namely, a segmentation fault.

The current value of a variable in a particular dimension can be represented graphically by a scrollbar (or a slider). We will discuss only scrollbars; the same idea can be extended to sliders as well.

The current interface of the WidgetKit class for scrollbars looks like this:

```
class WidgetKit {
  public:
    ...
    virtual Glyph* hscroll_bar(Adjustable*) const;
    ...
    virtual Glyph* vscroll_bar(Adjustable*) const;
    ...
    virtual Glyph* scroll_bar_look(DimensionName,
                                   Adjustable*) const = 0;
    ...
};
```

In this interface `hscroll_bar` always uses the `Dimension_X` of the Adjustable and returns a horizontal scrollbar. Similarly, `vscroll_bar` always uses the `Dimension_Y` of the Adjustable and returns a vertical scrollbar. The only method in which one can specify the `DimensionName` for an Adjustable is `scroll_bar_look`. But if we look at the implementation of this method, we see that it handles only the cases of `Dimension_X` and `Dimension_Y`, for which it returns a horizontal and vertical scrollbar respectively.

This clearly indicates our limitations. With the current interface, the following problems are visible:

- No dimension other than the `Dimension_X` and `Dimension_Y` can be graphically represented by a scrollbar.

- One cannot represent `Dimension_X` of an Adjustable through a vertical scrollbar. Similarly, `Dimension_Y` cannot be represented by a horizontal scrollbar. This functionality might be needed where one has more than two dimensions for an Adjustable and one needs to represent all these dimensions horizontally or vertically.

THE PROPOSED SOLUTIONS

Having identified two problems that don't allow the handling of multiple dimensions with an Adjustable, we now propose some solutions.

The Solution to the Adjustable Class Problem

The most obvious solution in this case is that the client of an Adjustable should be able to specify the number of dimensions that it wants for a given adjustable. Thus, there should be another Adjustable constructor that takes the number of dimensions, n, as an argument. Depending on this value of n, the array `AdjustableInfo info_` should be created.

The Solution to the WidgetKit Class Problem
The WidgetKit class interface should be general enough to handle the cases mentioned in the problems section. Thus, we propose the following extension to the interface of the WidgetKit class:

```
class WidgetKit {
  public:
    virtual Glyph* hscroll_bar(Adjustable*,
                               DimensionName d=Dimension_X) const;
    virtual Glyph* vscroll_bar(Adjustable*,
                               DimensionName d=Dimension_Y) const;

    virtual Glyph* scroll_bar_look(DimensionName,
                                   Adjustable*) const = 0;
    virtual Glyph* hscroll_bar_look(DimensionName,
                                    Adjustable*) const = 0;
    virtual Glyph* vscroll_bar_look(DimensionName,
                                    Adjustable*) const = 0;

    ...
};
```

In this interface for a `hscroll_bar`, one can also specify the dimension of the given Adjustable for which a horizontal scrollbar is required. Similarly, a vertical scrollbar can be created for any dimension of the Adjustable by using the `vscroll_bar` interface. If no dimension is specified for these methods, they behave just like the original `hscroll_bar` and `vscroll_bar` methods.

Two new methods, `hscroll_bar_look` and `vscroll_bar_look`, have been added so that a horizontal or vertical scrollbar can be created for any dimension of an Adjustable.

THE CHANGES REQUIRED

The implementation of the preceding solutions requires some changes in the interface of some other classes. We will look at these changes now.

The WidgetKit Interface
Other than the changes already mentioned, the method

```
    virtual Stepper* up_mover(Adjustable*) const;
```

should be extended to

```
    virtual Stepper* up_mover(Adjustable*, DimensionName d=Dimension_Y) const;
```

This ensures that a stepper at the end of a scrollbar can be used for any dimension for which its scrollbar area is being used.

Similarly, `down_mover`, `left_mover`, and `right_mover` are also extended. The default value of `DimensionName` for `up_mover` and `down_mover` is `Dimension_Y`, and for `left_mover` and `right_mover` is `Dimension_X`.

The Slider Interface

For the implementation of horizontal and vertical scrollbars, InterViews declares two subclasses of Slider class. These subclasses are class XSlider and YSlider. The XSlider creates a horizontal slider area in the scrollbar for `Dimension_X` while the YSlider provides vertical slider area in the scrollbar for `Dimension_Y` of the given Adjustable.

This limits the representation of dimensions of an Adjustable to only two dimensions: `Dimension_X` and `Dimension_Y`. To ensure that other dimensions can also be represented by scrollbars and that any dimension can be represented by a vertical or horizontal scrollbar, we create two subclasses of Slider class. These subclasses are known as HSlider and VSlider. The constructors of these classes are shown here:

```
HSlider(Style*, Adjustable*, DimensionName);
VSlider(Style*, Adjustable*, DimensionName);
```

The protocol of `Slider::allot_thumb_major_axis` should be extended so that it takes an additional argument. This last argument specifies the horizontal or vertical direction along which the major axis of the given slider is oriented. If no direction is specified, then an undefined direction is used and the method works just like the original one.

Xlib

The creation of this tool was also obstructed by some entities other than InterViews. The most notable of these is Xlib.

The Problem

After implementing our design, we observed that the response of *ice* was very slow. After running it through *prof*, we found the routines `_XcmsSquareRoot` and `_XcmsArcTangent` to be the culprits. The execution times of these two routines were sometimes as high as 80 percent of the total time. These routines are called from the color-conversion routines of Xlib. Discussion with Bob Scheifler about this issue revealed that Xlib does not use the `math` library routines for functions like `cosine`, `sine`, `tangent`, and so on. Instead, it provides its own implementation of these functions. These functions were much slower than their `math` library counterparts.

The Solution

We provided our own implementation of the two routines `_XcmsSquareRoot` and `_XcmsCubeRoot`. We created a new file, *XcmsMath.c*, and instead of the implementation provided by the Xlib version of these routines, we invoked the corresponding `math` library routines. For example, our implementation of `_XcmsSquareRoot` looks like this:

```
double _XcmsSquareRoot(a)
double a;
{
    return sqrt(a);
}
```

We also provided the `math` library implementation of the routines `_XcmsCosine`, `_XcmsSine`, and `_XcmsArcTangent` in the file *XcmsTrig.c*. Two object files were created for these two C files, and these object files were replaced in the Xlib. This library was then used to create the executable for *ice*.

The response of our tool improved appreciably with this solution.

INTERVIEWS VERSUS ATHENA WIDGETS

One of the central goals of this work is to gain insight into the strengths and weaknesses of Xt and the InterViews toolkits. This is a difficult but interesting proposition because the systems are so different. Why do we compare InterViews with Xt/Athena and not, say, Xt/Motif? While it is true that Motif contains more functionality than Athena, we felt that the comparison should focus more on the underlying systems than on GUIs. Also, we wanted to limit our consideration to freely available software because improvements attributable to the financial resources of commercial establishments were not considered germane to the essential worth of the base technologies. Our task here is to find some common criteria for comparison. Both systems show a number of strengths and weaknesses. We have subdivided the areas of comparison into eight categories: architecture, rendering, portability and code size, subclassing and inheritance, geometry management, event management, and resource management.

ARCHITECTURE

Both systems draw a line between their internal components and the components one sees on the screen, but they do so in different places. This is shown in Figure 3.

The mechanism/policy organizational dichotomy of Xt is well known. InterViews separates its core from look and feel issues by separating the world into the glyph hierarchy and kits. Kits are class factories that produce visible components. The largest architectural difference between the two systems is that in Xt the composite hierarchy resides mostly above the line or in the widget library, whereas in InterViews the composite management takes place entirely below the line in the TeX abstractions of the layout kit.

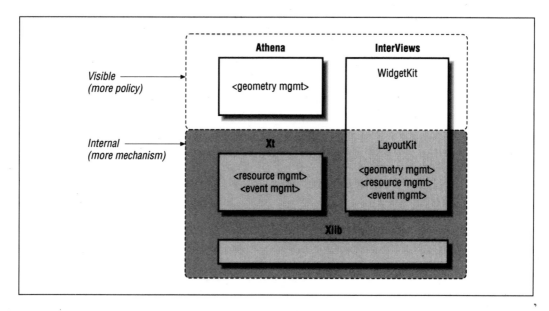

FIGURE 3: *THE ARCHITECTURE OF XT AND INTERVIEWS*

RENDERING

Both toolkits use a different target drawable for their base components at the Xlib layer. Xt widgets generally render to an X window, whereas InterViews glyphs render to an X window Region.[†]

Not maintaining a window per object allows InterViews to support many more objects than are used in a typical Xt application. The best example of this is the document editing program *doc*. By using a glyph per character, documents of over 185,000 separate C++ objects can be easily supported [13]. InterViews and Xt also differ in that widgets typically render directly to an X window, whereas InterViews glyphs render to an intermediate object known as a Canvas. Canvas is an object that supports a structured graphics protocol similar to the PostScript language. InterViews also supports a subclass of Canvas that supports hard-copy output. There is no equivalent to this in Xt.

PORTABILITY AND CODE SIZE

InterViews and Xt applications build on numerous platforms. However, InterViews maintains a porting layer between window systems not present in Xt. Providing this division of

---

† We are intentionally not considering gadgets. They were added to Xt as an afterthought. We are also not considering InterViews components that contain X windows—namely, Interactor and GLContext. These are exceptions to the rule.

code helps to ensure that any investment in application code will be preserved when we move on the next window system, whatever that may be.

Certainly the size of an applications source code has something to say about the complexity of expression in the toolkit. *ace* consists of 844 lines of source code.[†] *ice* is comprised of 1561 lines. These numbers would appear to be in Xt's favor. The *ice* programs design should probably be restudied with an eye toward reducing the number of its abstractions and the code to implement it.

Shared libraries have made executable size a less pressing issue than it once was. However, until memory is free, we will have to live with some constraints. On a Sun-4 processor running SunOS 4.1.2, *ace* took up 32,768 bytes, while *ice* consumed 90,112. Again these numbers favor Xt, although we expect that over time the continual improvement of C++ compilers will narrow this.

SUBCLASSING AND INHERITANCE

Subclassing and inheritance is the area in which Xt is the most severely deficient. The lack of object-oriented facilities in C leaves the task of implementing subclasses in the hands of the component designer. This can be a very tedious and error-prone process. Consider the following two code fragments, which compare subclassing in Xt and InterViews/C++.

```
C++:
class Foo : public  SuperFoo (MultipleInheritanceSuperFoo) {
  // lots of stuff
};
Xt:
typedef struct _FooClassPart {
  int ignore;
} FooClassPart;

typedef struct _FooClassRec {
  CoreClassPart core_class;
    . . .
  SuperFooClassPart super_foo_class;
  FooClassPart foo_class;
} FooClassRec;

typedef struct FooPart {
  /* lots of stuff */
} FooPart;

typedef struct _FooRec {
```

---

† The result of adding up the *.h*, *.c*, and *.ad* files.

```
    CorePart core;

      ...

    SuperFooPart superfoo;
    FooPart foo;
  } FooRec;
```

To perform a single subclassing operation in Xt, one must declare four C types. By comparison, in using InterViews one must be concerned with only a single C++ class declaration.

While the mechanism for subclassing in Xt is more complex, the options available to the programmer who wants to use its inheritance are very limited. To inherit a method, the widget designer must provide a special constant in the class field for that method. This is usually _XtInherit cast to an appropriate type. These kinds of details are hidden from the C++ class designer by the compiler. When one subclasses in C++, the default is for inheritance to be implicit. Xt supports only single inheritance, whereas C++ provides multiple inheritance. InterViews, as well as *ice*, takes advantage of this feature. Although multiple inheritance creates considerable complexity, it also assists in developing our applications to model the real world [8]. One of the most powerful mechanisms available to the C++ programmer is the virtual member function. These functions allow the programmer to pass a pointer to an object of a derived class into a context where only the interface of the base class is known, and to expect that the derived classes member function will be executed. This is also known as *polymorphism*, one of the keys to programming in C++. It is much more difficult to conceive of doing something analogous in Xt. First of all, a widget programmer is not supposed to access Xt methods outside a widget's .c file. Instead, widget implementations provide external or public functions that allow applications to use methods. Indeed, there is no widget code ever written that we are aware of that passes around and manipulates a widget pointer with anything near the flexibility achieved with a C++ class pointer. While one can implement polymorphism in Xt, we are not sure one would want to. The programmer would have to be very careful. For example, one could write a function (internal to a widget's implementation, of course) that accepted a generic widget pointer to a subclass of Composite and then invoked its insert_child method. If you were to do this, you had better be sure you have implemented this function and filled in the appropriate class part field with its address; otherwise you would be committing a serious programming error. C++, by comparison, guarantees that invoking a subclasses member function will resolve to an actual function; otherwise the program simply will not compile.

Both systems differ as to when they implement their inheritance. For Xt, inheritance for a subclass occurs during run time when the first widget of the given subclass is dynamically created. Encountering the _XtInherit constant tells a class to pull a method function pointer out of the appropriate field in its superclass record and place it in the subclass. This is known as *class part initialization*. By contrast, C++ defines inheritance at compilation and link time, through a number of stratagems [9]. This enables the C++ compiler to check the class structure for correctness, as well as for performing optimizations such as class flattening [10].

Xt does, however, have a feature not present in C++. Fields can be added to a class record without recompilation of the application through the use of an extension class record. No such mechanism exists in C++, where the addition of a class member mandates recompilation.

GEOMETRY MANAGEMENT

We can divide geometry management into three categories: (1) structure, or how the system organizes aggregates of components; (2) layout, or how user interface objects are initially placed when the application is displayed on the screen; and (3) reconfigurability, or how the system reorganizes subcomponents when one or more of them want to change their size.

STRUCTURE

Creating components to physically manage subcomponents is accomplished in Xt through subclassing from the Composite and Constraint widget classes. Their architecture is as follows.

Composite class:

```
typedef struct _CompositeClassRec {
    CoreClassPart  core_class;
    CompositeClassPart composite_class;
} CompositeClassRec;

typedef struct _CompositeClassPart {
  XtGeometryHandler geometry_manager;
  XtWidgetProc      change_managed;
  XtArgsProc        insert_child;
  XtWidgetProc      delete_child;
  caddr_t           extension;
} CompositeClassPart;

typedef struct _CompositeRec {
    CorePart core;
    CompositePart composite;
} CompositeRec;

typedef struct _CompositePart {
    WidgetList children;             /* list of children */
    Cardinal num_children;        /* number on list */
    Cardinal num_slots;          /* max size of list */
    XtOrderProc insert_position;        /* method */
} CompositePart;
```

Constraint class:

```
typedef struct _ConstraintClassRec {
    CoreClassPart      core_class;
    CompositeClassPart composite_class;
    ConstraintClassPart constraint_class;
} ConstraintClassRec;


typedef struct _ConstraintClassPart {
    XtResourceList resources;    /* constraint resource list */
    Cardinal num_resources;      /* number of 'em */
    Cardinal constraint_size;    /* size of the constraint struct */
    XtInitProc initialize;       /* method */
    XtWidgetProc destroy;        /* method */
    XtSetValuesFunc set_values;  /* method */
    caddr_t extension;
} ConstraintClassPart;

typedef struct _ConstraintRec {
    CorePart core;
    CompositePart composite;
    ConstraintPart constraint;
} ConstraintRec *ConstraintWidget;

typedef struct _ConstraintPart {
    int *empty;
} ConstraintPart;
```

Conceptually, composite widgets are containers that usually have been given the responsibility for maintaining their children in a uniform fashion. All widgets must ask their parents to make changes such as resize or movement. A number of widget methods accomplish this, such as `InsertChild`, `DeleteChild`, `Resize`, `QueryGeometry`, `GeometryManager`, and `ChangeManaged`. Constraint widgets, by comparison, are a subclass of Composite that differ in that management is based on additional information associated with each child. This information is found in a constraint structure that is pointed to by a field of the CorePart of a widgets instance record.

There are 15 widgets in the Athena library that subclass from Composite or Composite along with Constraint. All of them are abstractions of common containers we find in the real world. They are Box, Dialog, Form, Paned, Porthole, Tree, Viewport, and various shells. By contrast, the geometry management paradigm of InterViews is far more complex. In addition to the goal of simple containers, the goal of InterViews is to geometrically handle full text-formatting functionality along the lines of Donald Knuth's TeX system [11]. As in TeX, Boxes and Glue are the conceptual objects that the basic rendering object or glyph is organized by. Composite components in InterViews are created by invoking member functions of the LayoutKit class. Kits can be viewed as software factories that organize the dispensing of objects. An abbreviated list of LayoutKit's composite objects include box, overlay, deck, back, front, glue, discretionary, strut, space, center, fixed, flexible, natural, margin, stretch, and span. LayoutKit also includes nine member functions, all of which heavily reflect the needs of document formatting. We would argue that the InterViews model is superior, because the page-layout model subsumes the simpler model of Xt and Athena. This allows for more sophisticated schemes of geometry management.

LAYOUT

The Placement of objects in Xt occurs throughout the phases of widget creation, management, and finally realization. In the creation phase, after all the widgets have invoked their `class_initialize` methods, widgets whose parents are Constraints have a constraint record allocated and its address stored away. If a widget's parent is a composite, the intrinsics puts itself into its parent's children list by calling the parent's `insert_child` method. *Management* is the process by which lists of widgets are added to the geometry managed set of their parent Composite. *Realization* is the process of creating a widget's X window to the screen. After a series of calls to create widgets and manage subtrees, an application has a tree of unrealized widgets, some of which are managed and some of which are not. Composite realization is achieved by invoking the `change_managed` method for each child of a composite with any managed children. This is done in recursive postorder. Therefore, layout starts at the leaves of the composite hierarchy and works upward. This lets layout algorithms know what the preferred size of the children should be. Changes can ripple up and down the tree, but since a widget can not request new geometry as a result of being resized, the process is guaranteed to eventually terminate. We should note here that creating but not managing widgets is a useful technique by which the Xt applications programmer can create large structures, such as menus, before really needing them, and then quickly display them on the screen. No comparable mechanism exists in Interviews.

The InterViews layout system is quite different in nature. Glyph layout and rendering takes place in three phases, corresponding to three member functions. We will call these the requisition, Allocation, and drawing phases. These phases correspond to the three glyph member functions `Glyph::request`, `Glyph::allocate`, and `Glyph::draw`.

- Requisition phase: In the first phase, glyphs make their space needs known. The outermost glyph has its request member invoked, passing in a Requisition object. Requisition objects contain information such as how much space a glyph needs and how much they are willing to compromise by shrinking or stretching. Container glyphs call the request members of their children to compute their Requisitions, which are stored away for later.

- Allocation phase: In the second phase, the outermost glyph has its allocate member function invoked, passing in an Allocation object. Allocations contain the size of a glyph that is actually given. Container glyphs call the allocate members of their children and use the previously stored Requisition information to compute their Allocation. This information is also stored away.

- Drawing phase: In the third and final phase, the outermost glyphs draw member is invoked, passing it a Canvas object as well as an Allocation. Container glyphs invoke the draw members of their children, causing them to be drawn on the Canvas by using the geometry information saved in the Allocation.

We find the InterViews system to be more symmetrical and elegant. Again C++ assists here. Geometry management is a matter of mixing functionality with information, and language support of this in the implementation of the Requisition and Allocation classes is superior.

RECONFIGURABILITY

Both systems support the notion of adding and deleting a child from its parent aggregate. Xt defines two methods in the Composite widget class to do this: `InsertChild` and `Delete-Child`. InterViews accomplishes this through six member functions in the Glyph class: `append`, `prepend`, `insert`, `remove`, `replace`, and `change`. Again we see that the Inter-Views mechanism subsumes the Xt model.

Both systems provide flexibility when a child's geometry needs conflict with the parent's management policy. In Xt this is accomplished through the child's invocation of the parent's GeometryManager method. The parent can return XtGeometryYes, in which case the child can resize. Returning `XtGeometryDone` to the child means that Xt has already accomplished the resize. `XtGeometryNo` constitutes a denial of the request.

InterViews dictates reconfigurability through the alignment operations of the Layout kit. These operations affect a glyphs Requisition. `Layout::center` aligns a glyphs origin in the request/allocate process described earlier. `Layout::fixed` make glyphs ridged and unresizable. `Layout::flexible` makes them stretchable and shrinkable. Margins can also be specified. User interface objects can be managed like characters in a formatting system by using the Discretionary, Composition, and Compositor classes. While all of these techniques create a flexible system for the GUI designer, the text formatter paradigm will present a certain learning curve to the vast majority of engineers who grew up using the management technique found in the more traditional Xt widget libraries.

EVENT MANAGEMENT

Events constitute the dynamic aspect of window systems. The X Window System defines 17 basic event types, but this number belies the complexity of event management. Therefore, it is essential to provide good tools for organizing an application's reactions to the events delivered. Before toolkits arrived, event programming in the X Window System consisted of nothing more than creating a C switch statement in the main event loop of a program. Both InterViews and Xt have the notion of event structure. Of course, Xt simply uses the XEvent structure, while InterViews provides a window system–independent abstraction called the Event class. In Xt, one abstracts the event loop by providing a series of functions known as event handlers and registering them with the intrinsics by using the XtAddEventHandler function. InterViews provides the Handler class to effect event management. Handlers are objects that are passed an event to process in much the same way as Xt event handlers.

However, InterViews provides some interesting subclasses of Handler that provide additional functionality. InputHandlers provide the programmer with a highly configurable focus management system for mouse and keyboard input. Essentially, you are provided with a tree structure of input objects and a mechanism for traversing that tree. The class protocol allows you to change focus by traversing the tree. InputHandlers take up physical space and participate in the Allocation protocol. InputHandlers share with the Patch class an ability to cause layout to change by invoking their redraw member. Indeed, `InputHandler::redraw` and `Patch::redraw` are important member functions in that they effect "damage" on the canvas where glyphs are being drawn. Damage in InterViews is the mechanism by which glyphs are redrawn. In order to redraw a glyph, you damage an object known as an *extension*, which comprises the geometry of the glyph on the canvas. Extensions are initialized in the glyph allocation phase. Canvas damage is somewhat analogous to the `expose` widget method in Xt, except it would not be unreasonable to use this technique in your application instead of merely refreshing a window. It is indeed possible for no damage to occur when an obscured InterViews application is popped to the front of a window stack. Characters do not damage the canvas when they are exposed. Resizing an application that contains a slider will cause damage to the canvas because the size of the thumb needs to change.

Although InterViews presents some good ideas, Xt maintains a performance edge through its tighter coupling with the X system. Clients can request that the server compress its motion events, generating them only when the pointer starts or stops moving. Such granularity of control would violate InterViews X independence but results in slower programs.

Both systems provide the ability to react to file IO and to invoke functions based on the expiration of a timer. Xt does this by registering input handlers and timeout proc's with the functions `XtAppAddInputHandler` and `XtAppAddTimeOut`. Xt input handlers are useful specifically in designing graphical interfaces for standard Unix utilities [12]. InterViews provides these mechanisms through the IOHandler class—namely, the `inputReady`, `outputReady`, and `timerExpired` members. Xt, however, provides the capability to use time that would otherwise be lost waiting for events by registering work procedures through the `XtAppAddWorkProc` function call. No such mechanism is available in InterViews.

Another major strength of Xt over InterViews is the translation table, an action procedure mechanism made available through the Intrinsics resources. Using this, you can write a number of functions that perform various jobs, and bind them at run time to various events. As with workprocs, InterViews provides no such capability.

Xt's translation table can be useful in designing graphical interfaces for standard Unix utilities [12]. Xt provides the `XtAddInput()` call. InterViews provides the Dispatcher class. Both systems handle timeouts and workprocs. InterViews lacks a notion of translation tables and accelerators. This is bad. Also, InterViews has no notion of selections, although this is currently being considered.

RESOURCE MANAGEMENT

Resource management is an area in which Xt and InterViews differ substantially. While the InterViews paradigm is organized in a substantially different manner from that of Xt, we are not convinced that it is superior.

The major conceptual difference between the systems is that the Xt resource system is built around the physical organization of an application, whereas InterViews has chosen to create a separate or logical hierarchy. Whereas physical structure in an InterViews application is embodied in its glyph hierarchy, logical or resource structure is managed by a separate class known as a Style.

Xt's resource mechanism has proven itself in the real world and is a major reason for the toolkits success. It starts with the Xrm calls available in Xlib, and gives the application programmer substantial functionality by simply incorporating a certain widget into the application and setting its resources. Both toolkits allow the user to provide resources on the command line and in a database file.[†]

Both systems support the notion of resource converters. Xt allows resources to dynamically change through invoking a widget's `SetValues` method, whereas InterViews implements this through the Styles trigger member function.[‡]

Despite these similarities, we see substantial differences. Programmers using widgets simply add them to their program and begin to use their resources. To affect a component in InterViews, one must link the physical kit component with its logical style component in order to reach it with attributes stored in a resource file. Yes, this is more flexible, but it makes for more work. Indeed, InterViews resource management is quite a bit more complex than that of Xt. You need to understand and be comfortable with only two concepts to use Xt resources: *class* and *instance*. InterViews causes you to become familiar with *Styles*, the distinction between *physical* and *logical hierarchies*, a style's *name*, style *prefixes*, *attributes*, and finally *aliases*. Many GUI programmers who have had great success with Xt resources are not going to be pleased with the complexity of the new system.

The designers of InterViews assert that the tight coupling between customizable attributes and the layout of objects in Xt is useless for objects such as documents, where attributes apply to logical rather than physical groupings [14]. While this may be so, we are not yet convinced that the document-formatting paradigm is best. What other application domains would this approach provide leverage in? Monitoring nuclear power plants? Games? Database management? The abstraction seems to be overkill for 90 percent of the toolkit application domain. Indeed, in the document formatting business, there are very successful products such as FrameMaker that use traditional Xt mechanisms with no difficulty.

---

† Although to date, while Xt supports the *, ., and ? pattern-matching constructs, InterViews supports only *.

‡ This has not yet been implemented.

Finally, it is claimed by the InterViews designers that, by dividing up functionality that toolkits have traditionally coupled, InterViews is able to provide a unified framework for user preferences, document attributes, and a structured graphics state that should make applications simpler to build, more consistent to use, and easier to integrate [14]. While some good evidence has been provided for this in the case of the *doc* program, there is no major application that shows this for structured graphics.[†]

There is not enough evidence that the style methodology creates a resource design environment that is simpler and more consistent. Whether it is easier to integrate depends on what you are trying to integrate it with. Certainly not Xt programs. It would not have been difficult to incorporate the Xt mechanism into InterViews. One could have used Xrm to provide resource setting through a physical and logical hierarchy. Sometimes it is unnecessary to reinvent the wheel.

CONCLUSION

This paper has described the design and implementation of two color editors, *ace* and *ice*, written in the Athena/Xt and InterViews toolkits. At present, two versions of *ice* exist. The first version has been implemented using the changes that we have suggested in InterViews. In our local environment, using Sun workstations and cfront, they seem to work fine. These changes are also upward-compatible, so that any code written using the old interface also works.

The second version of *ice* has been implemented using InterViews 3.1 as it is. It and *ace* have been made publicly available by anonymous ftp on *export.lcs.mit.edu* in the file */contrib/ACEvsICE.tar.Z*.

Various aspects of the InterViews design were examined during the design of this tool. Their advantages and disadvantages were discussed between us. The changes that we have proposed in this paper were sent to Mark Linton, and the handling of multiple dimensions could be supported in the full release of InterViews 3.1.

The documentation available for InterViews is still somewhat scarce. More detailed documentation should be made available. Also, there are not enough examples that can be used as a model to develop custom applications. Thus, for an InterViews novice, programming in InterViews seems like an uphill battle. We hope that, as more people adopt InterViews as their user interface library, good examples and documentation will become prolific.

---

† InterViews 3.1 contains a glyph editor, but this application is just a toy.

BIBLIOGRAPHY

[1] J. D. Foley, A. van Dam, S. K. Feiner, and J. F. Hughes, *Computer Graphics Principles and Practice*, 2d ed., Addison-Wesley, Reading, MA, 1990.

[2] M. A. Linton, P. R. Calder, J. A. Interrante, S. Tang, and J. M. Vlissides, *InterViews Reference Manual Version 3.1-Beta*, June 26, 1992.

[3] R. W. Scheifler, "What's New in Release 5," *THE X RESOURCE*, Issue 0, Fall 1991, O'Reilly & Associates, pp. 7–16.

[4] A. Tabayoyon and J. M. Taylor, "Xcms: Integrated Color Management for X11," Tutorial Notes, Xhibition '91, June 5, 1991.

[5] J. M. Taylor and A. Tabayoyon, "An Introduction to Device-Independent Color and Color Management," Tutorial Notes, 6th X Technical Conference, Jan 13, 1992.

[6] "TekColor Color Management System," *System Implementor's Manual*, March 1990, Tektronix, Beaverton, OR.

[7] TIFF, Revision 6.0, Final Q, June 3, 1992, Aldus Developers Desk, Aldus Corporation, Seattle, WA.

[8] S. Myers, *Effective C++*, Addison-Wesley, 1992, pp. 157–169.

[9] B. Stroustrup and M. Ellis, *The Annotated C++ Reference Manual*, Addison-Wesley, 1990, pp. 217–237.

[10] I. Bashi and U. Bellur, "A Class Flattening Tool," Conference Proceedings, C++ at Work 1991, Nov 18, 1991.

[11] D. Knuth, *The Texbook*, Addison-Wesley, 1984.

[12] D. Young, *X Window Systems Programming and Applications with Xt*, Prentice Hall, 1989, pp. 142–151.

[13] P. Calder and M. Linton, "The Object-Oriented Implementation of a Document Editor." Unpublished.

[14] P. Calder and M. Linton, "Managing Attributes in a User Interface Toolkit." Unpublished.

[15] W. Lalonde and J. Pugh, *Inside Smalltalk Volume II*, Prentice Hall, 1991, pp. 7–12.

[16] Palay et al., "The Andrew Toolkit: An Overview," The Andrew Project: Selected Technical Papers, Information Technology Center, CMU, 1990.

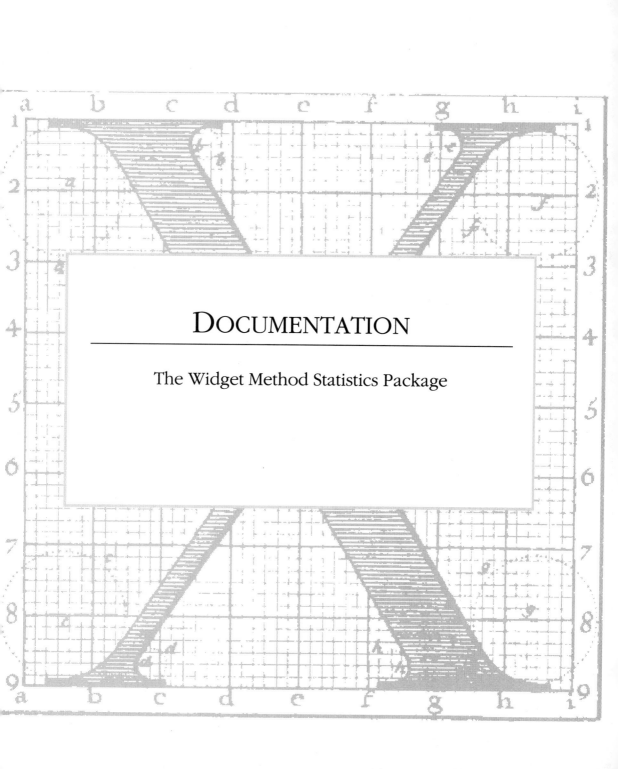

DOCUMENTATION

The Widget Method Statistics Package

THE WIDGET METHOD STATISTICS PACKAGE
TABLE OF CONTENTS

THE WIDGET METHOD STATISTICS PACKAGE:

TOOLS FOR MONITORING AND MEASURING METHOD USAGE

Bruce Gendler

ABSTRACT

This paper describes a set of tools that application and widget developers can use to trace, and collect performance statistics on, the core class methods of any widget class. The trace capability allows a developer to see, as a program is running, output that shows the invocation of each method called by the Xt Intrinsics. The statistics capability gathers, while a program is running, statistics that can later be analyzed using utility programs provided as part of the package. Program profilers may be able to report statistics such as the number of times a routine is called and the amount of time spent in that routine, but they cannot distinguish between different calls to the same routine. The tools presented in this paper allow a developer to quantify the performance overhead of methods down to the level of a specific widget instance.

Bruce Gendler is a Senior Computer Scientist/Department Manager for Computer Sciences Corporation. He is currently working on the development of workstation-based applications to generate, display, and manipulate meteorological images, graphics, and data. He got his B.S. at Brandeis University and his M.S. from George Washington University, both in computer science. Bruce can be reached by email (bgendler@csc.com) or at CSC, 3160 Fairview Park Dr., Falls Church, Virginia, 22042.

INTRODUCTION

An important characteristic of all Xt Intrinsics–based widgets is that they are opaque. That is, the data structures and code that comprise a widget class are hidden from the application developer using it, and are visible only to the developer of the widget class. Application developers access these data structures and code through mechanisms provided by the Xt Intrinsics (e.g., `XtVaSetValues()`) or the author of the widget class (e.g., `XmListSelectItem()`). This means that applications based on widgets are using data structures and code that they cannot access directly. Of course, this is the intent of the Xt Intrinsics and the object-oriented nature of widgets. It does mean, however, that widget-based applications are composed largely of code that the application developer has a limited understanding of and no control over.

All widget classes are subclasses of the Core widget class and therefore have a set of Core class methods associated with them. Some of these methods can be NULL, and others can be inherited from a superclass. In every case, though, a widget class implements some of its own Core class methods. Methods are called by other methods or by the Xt Intrinsics based on behavior defined in the Xt Intrinsics specification. Each method is called for a different reason: some in response to X events (Expose) and others in response to Xt Intrinsics–defined events (widget creation, geometry management requests, set values, and so on). The manner in which methods are called varies as well. Some are chained from superclass to subclass, one (the destroy method) is chained from subclass to superclass, and others are not chained at all.

None of this is intuitive. Fortunately, understanding these concepts is not a prerequisite for writing Xt Intrinsics–based applications. They are concepts, however, that must be understood before you can develop new widgets and optimize applications. The package of tools presented in this paper were designed to provide insight into the behavior of the Xt Intrinsics and into the overhead imposed by widget methods on an application.

The next section describes the monitoring capabilities of the Widget Method Statistics (WMS) package.

MONITORING METHODS USING THE WMS PACKAGE

The WMS package performs method tracing and statistics collection. These capabilities are activated by incorporating calls to the WMS subroutine `XwmsSelectMethod()` in your application. This routine is passed a widget class and a methods mask that indicates which methods should be monitored. For example, the following call would be used to activate monitoring of the `initialize`, `expose`, `set_values` methods of the XmPushButton widget class:

```
XwmsSelectMethod (xmPushButtonWidgetClass, InitializeMask |
ExposeMask | SetValuesMask);
```

Calls to `XwmsSelectMethod()` can be made anywhere in the application. To usefully monitor methods that are called only when widgets are created, such as `class_initialize`, `class_part_initialize`, `initialize`, and `initialize_hook`, calls to `XwmsSelectMethod()` must be made before widget creation. Monitoring can be selectively turned off by calling the `XwmsDeselectMethod()` subroutine.

Once method monitoring has been activated, tracing and statistics collection take place automatically. Method tracing is displayed to standard output, and statistics are written to a file called the WMS database. WMS report applications can then be used to analyze the WMS database. The following sections describe the trace capability and reporting tools in more detail.

WIDGET METHOD TRACING

The widget method tracing capability was designed to show the calling sequence of methods as a program operates. As the program executes, trace output for the selected methods and widget classes is continually issued. This rather verbose stream of output can be analyzed as the program is executing (interactively), or it can be saved to a file and analyzed later. When used interactively, it allows the user to perform an action and immediately see what methods are called and in what order, in response to that action.

Each line of trace data indicates that a particular method was entered, and contains the following information:

- Method name: This is the name of the method that was called. It is one of the fifteen Core class methods.

- Method class: This is the widget class that the method belongs to. This is important because there are cases in which the widget class of the method being executed is not the same as the class passed to the method or of the widget class of the widget passed to it. This concept will become clearer in the next section, which describes specific examples of trace output.

- Widget name: This is the name of the widget passed to the method. For the `class_initialize` and `class_part_initialize` methods this field is blank.

- Widget class: This is the name of the widget class of the widget passed to the method. For the `class_initialize` method this field is blank. For the `class_part_initialize` method it indicates which widget class is having its subpart initialized.

TRACE EXAMPLES

The examples contained in this section demonstrate what can be learned by simply viewing the trace output of a simple Xt Intrinsics–based program. The specification describes, in great detail, the required behavior of the Intrinsics. The trace output of the WMS package provides tangible data that can be used to better understand the concepts described in that specification.

Each example shows a different portion of trace output produced by the same program. The first two examples directly correlate to behavior described in the Xt specification. The first example shows the Xt Intrinsics use of the `class_initialize` and `class_part_initialize` methods. The second example shows how the `resize` and `expose` methods are invoked in response to the user resizing a shell. The third example, specific to the Motif XmPushButton widget class, shows the use of methods invoked from action procedures in response to the user selecting a push button. These examples solidified my understanding of concepts that I had only read about before.

The code for this program can be found in Appendix A at the end of this paper. The program is a simple Motif program that contains a shell widget with a push button as a child. Tracing for all methods of the Xt Intrinsics Application Shell and the Motif XmPushButton and Label classes has been activated by using XwmsSelectMethod in the following manner:

```
XwmsSelectMethod (xmLabelWidgetClass, AllMethodsMask);
XwmsSelectMethod (xmPushButtonWidgetClass, AllMethodsMask);
XwmsSelectMethod (applicationShellWidgetClass, AllMethodsMask);
```

The constant `AllMethodsMask` indicates that all methods of the class are to be monitored. Notice that there is a call for the Label widget class because Label is the superclass of PushButton and we are interested in tracing superclass methods as well.

EXAMPLE 1: THE CLASS_PART_INITIALIZE METHOD

The first example, the `class_part_initialize` method, illustrates the sequence of class and instance initialization methods that are called the first time that an instance of a widget class is created. In this sample program, these methods are called in response to the program calling XtVaCreateManagedWidget to create the XmPushButton widget.

The first time a widget of a class is created, the Intrinsics ensures that the widget class and its superclasses are initialized in a superclass to subclass order. This can be seen in the following trace output by the calls to the `class_initialize` and `class_part_initialize` methods of the XmLabel and XmPushButton widget classes.

```
class_initialize(XmLabel): entered
class_part_initialize: (XmLabel) part of XmLabel: entered
class_initialize(XmPushButton): entered
class_part_initialize: (XmLabel) part of XmPushButton: entered
class_part_initialize: (XmPushButton) part of XmPushButton: entered
initialize.XmLabel for widget button.XmPushButton: entering
initialize.XmPushButton for widget button.XmPushButton: entering
```

Because class initialization is chained in a superclass-to-subclass direction, and because XmLabel is the first superclass of XmPushButton we have selected to have monitored, the first class we see being initialized in the trace output is the XmLabel widget class. Initializing the XmLabel widget class consists of first calling its `class_initialize` method and then calling the necessary `class_part_initialize` methods in a superclass-to- subclass order. In this example, since none of the XmLabel superclasses are being traced, only the call to the XmLabel `class_part_initialize` method appears in the trace output.

After initializing the XmLabel class, the Intrinsics then initializes the XmPushButton widget class. First, its `class_initialize` method is called. Then the `class_part_initialize` methods are called. Note that, since these are chained in a superclass-to- subclass order, the `class_part_initialize` method of the XmLabel class is called first, before the `class_part_initialize` method of the XmPushButton class. Also note that the first call to the XmLabel class `class_part_initialize` method is made to initialize the Label part of the XmLabel class record, and the second call to it is made to initialize the Label part of the XmPushButton class record.

After completing initialization of the widget class, the specific widget instance is initialized. The `initialize` method is one that is also chained in a superclass-to-subclass direction. This is shown by the two `initialize` method trace lines. The first line shows the `initialize` method of the XmLabel class being called for the button XmPushButton widget. The second line shows the `initialize` method of the XmPushButton widget class being called for the same widget.

EXAMPLE 2: THE RESIZE AND EXPOSE METHODS

The second example illustrates the sequence of methods that are called in a response to an application being resized. It provides insight into how the Intrinsics handle shell resizing and how XtResizeWidget() works. It also provides insight into the operation of the `resize` and `expose` methods of the XmPushButton widget class. Note the use of indentation to show cases in which one method directly calls another.

```
resize.ApplicationShell for widget test1.ApplicationShell: entering
    resize.XmPushButton for widget button.XmPushButton: entering
        resize.XmLabel for widget button.XmPushButton: entering
    expose.XmPushButton for widget button.XmPushButton: entering
        expose.XmLabel for widget button.XmPushButton: entering
```

The `resize` method of the ApplicationShell, created by the call to XtAppInitialize(), is called by the Intrinsics in response to the user resizing the application window. This method, inherited from a superclass of the ApplicationShell widget class, calls XtResize-Widget() for each of its managed children. In this case, the PushButton is its only managed child. XtResizeWidget() then calls the `resize` method of the XmPushButton widget class on behalf of the XmPushButton widget. This method, as part of its functionality, directly calls the `resize` method of its superclass, the XmLabel class.

After the resizing is complete, the widgets are exposed. The XmPushButton is the only widget that needs exposing. The `expose` method of the XmPushButton widget class is called by the Intrinsics. This method, as part of its functionality, directly calls the `expose` method of its superclass, the XmLabel class.

EXAMPLE 3: ACTIONS AND THE EXPOSE METHOD

The third example illustrates the case in which methods are called directly by an action procedure rather than by the Intrinsics or another method. It shows the trace output produced when the push button, an instance of the XmPushButton widget class, is selected and deselected.

```
expose.XmLabel for widget button.XmPushButton: entering
expose.XmLabel for widget button.XmPushButton: entering
```

The two lines are identical. The first corresponds to selecting the button; the second corresponds to deselecting the button. The fact that they reference the XmLabel expose method rather than the XmPushButton expose method was initially confusing to me. Then I realized that the XmPushButton action routines Arm and Activate, which are called when the button is selected and deselected, are both calling the expose method of the XmLabel class directly.

REPORTING APPLICATIONS

This section demonstrates how the WMS reporting applications can be used to gain insight into the effect of the Core class methods on the performance of an application. Three utilities are described: *wmsclass*, *wmsmethod*, and *wmswidget*. A fourth application, *wmsdump*, which is used for simply dumping the WMS database into a trace format, is not discussed.

WMS REPORTING EXAMPLES

The reports are generated for a test program, *test2.c*, which can be found in Appendix B at the end of this paper. This simple program displays a label and three push buttons. Two of the push buttons are used to increment and decrement the numeric value displayed in the label. The third push button is used to double the amount by which the numeric value is incremented and decremented. The program is run and the file *test2.stats* is created. The run consists of selecting each of the buttons multiple times and resizing the shell.

WMSCLASS

It is usually best to run *wmsclass* first. *Wmsclass* produces a report, for a specified widge-class, that shows the statistics for each of that class's Core class methods. To produce a report on the use of the XmPushButton Core class methods, you execute *wmsclass* in the following way:

```
% wmsclass -f test2.stats -c XmPushButton
```

The -f option indicates that the file *test2.stats* should be used as the source of data to generate the report. The -c option identifies the XmPushButton class as the one we want statistics for. Report 1 shows the output.

```
        Method Class: XmPushButton
       Produced By: wmsclass
        File Name: test2.stats
```

Method	Times Called	Secs	Nanosecs
class_initialize	1	0	16420864
class_part_initialize	1	0	90880
initialize	3	0	4226304
initialize_hook	0	0	0
realize	3	0	3171328
destroy	0	0	0
resize	5	0	17787136
expose	13	0	28908288
set_values	7	0	1186304
set_values_hook	0	0	0
set_values_almost	1	0	1302016
get_values_hook	0	0	0
accept_focus	0	0	0
query_geometry	0	0	0
display_accelerator	0	0	0

This report displays the number of times each method was called and the amount of time (in seconds and nanosecond) spent in each. You can see from the report that some methods were never called and that the expose method was called 13 times. This pattern of behavior is one that I have seen in almost every one of the programs that I have used with the WMS package. It certainly validates the assertion that the expose method is an important one and that it should be optimized and called as infrequently as possible. It is also interesting to notice the large amount of time spent in the one call to the class_initialize method relative to the other methods. This is not of great concern, however, because it is called only once per application.

WMSMETHOD

The *wmsmethod* utility can then be used to see how the 13 calls to the expose method were distributed between the three push buttons of the application. To produce the report shown in Report 2, you execute the *wmsmethod* as follows:

```
% wmsmethod -f test2.stats -m expose -c XmPushButton
```

The -m expose identifies the expose method, and the -c XmPushButton identifies XmPushButton as the widget class whose expose method we are interested in.

```
        Method Name: expose
       Widget Class: XmPushButton
        Produced By: wmsmethod
         File Name: test2.stats
```

```
Total Number of times called: 13
Total time in method: 0 sec 28908288 nanosecs
```

Widget	Widget Class	Times Called	Secs	Nanosecs
Decrement	XmPushButton	3	0	10288384
Increment	XmPushButton	3	0	5878016
Interval	XmPushButton	7	0	12741888

From this report we see that 7 of the 13 exposes were on behalf of the widget Interval. Interval is the push button used to change the amount that the counter is incremented and decremented by. This means that either this button was selected more frequently (causing its label to change each time) or that it was exposed from a fully or partially obscured state more often. From this report we can see also that the time spent exposing the Decrement widget was much larger than the time spent exposing the Increment widget even though both were called the same number of times. Since these two buttons are essentially the same, the difference may be due simply to the load on the system at the time of the exposures. Multiple runs followed by WMS analysis can be done to determine if this is a pattern, indicating something in the code, or just a function of the load on the system at the time the method is called. We can see also that the time spent exposing the Decrement widget was closer to that of the Interval widget than it was to that of the Increment widget even though the Interval widget was exposed more than twice as often.

WMSWIDGET

To look at all method usage for the Interval widget, use the *wmswidget* utility. This application produces the output shown in Report 3. It is invoked in the following way:

```
% wmswidget -f test2.stats -w Interval -c XmPushButton
```

The `-w Interval` identifies Interval as the widget, and `-c XmPushButton` identifies XmPushButton as the class whose methods will be reported for the Interval widget.

```
    Widget Name: Interval
   Method Class: XmPushButton
    Produced By: wmswidget
      File Name: test2.stats
```

Method	Times Called	Secs	Nanosecs
initialize	1	0	1519360
initialize_hook	0	0	0
realize	1	0	1025792
destroy	0	0	0
resize	1	0	1768960
expose	7	0	12741888

set_values	5	0	979712
set_values_hook	0	0	0
set_values_almost	1	0	1302016
get_values_hook	0	0	0
accept_focus	0	0	0
query_geometry	0	0	0
display_accelerator	0	0	0

From this report we see the method usage for the Interval push button. In addition to the seven executions of the expose method that we saw on the preceding *wmsmethod* report, we see also that, for the Interval widget, four methods were called once (initialize, realize, resize, and set_values_almost) and the set_values method was called five times. The five calls to the set_values method are a direct result of pressing the Interval button. The XmNactivateCallback() for this button changes the text in the button label when you use XtVaSetValues(). The single call to the set_values_almost method is in response to the size of the Interval button changing as the increment value displayed in it increases (that is, as more digits are needed).

WMS IMPLEMENTATION

This section describes how the WMS package performs the monitoring of methods. This monitoring can be divided into three distinct phases:

- WMS initialization
- Method selection and installation
- Method execution

The following subsections describe each of these. They are followed by a fourth section that describes what is required to monitor the methods of a custom widget class.

WMS INITIALIZATION

Initialization of the WMS package occurs implicitly when XwmsSelectMethod() is first called. There is no initialization subroutine in the WMS library. The sole purpose of initialization is to initialize data structures to support the monitoring of widget classes.

The WMS initialize routine sets up a linked list that contains one structure for each widget class that can be monitored. The contents of the linked list vary based on the widget set being used. The Motif version of the WMS package, for example, contains one structure for each Motif widget class. The Xt Intrinsics–supplied Application Shell widget class is included in all versions. The subroutine XwmsInstallWidgetClass() is provided so that custom widget classes can be added to the list and can be monitored.

Each of these widget-class structures contains pointers to special WMS methods, instead of the original widget-class methods, that are called during program execution. These methods are simple, one-line methods that call a corresponding Xwms method. The xmDrawingArea_expose method, for example, calls the _Xwms_expose method. The Xwms methods perform tracing and statistics collection, and call the original method. The following code example shows the one-line expose method for the XmDrawingArea widget class:

```
void xmDrawingArea_expose (w, event, region)
    Widget w;
    XEvent *event;
    Region region;
{
    _Xwms_expose (w, event, region, xmDrawingAreaWidgetClass);
}
```

In order to perform accurate statistics collection and to call the correct method, the WMS method (_Xwms_expose in this case) is passed one additional argument. This argument is the widget class of the method. It is used by the WMS software to locate the original method to be called and to properly document the trace information. This is necessary because the WMS statistics method cannot rely on the widget class of the widget passed to it to call the correct method. There are some cases in which the widget passed in is of one class but the method to be called is actually of a different class. An example of this is when the XmLabel Motif widge-class expose method gets called directly by the XmPushButton expose method. The widget passed to it is an instance of the XmPushButton class, not of the XmLabel class. There are other cases in which no widget is passed to a method at all. One example of this is the class_part_initialize method. A class's class_part_initialize method is called whenever one of its subclasses is performing class initialization. It is passed the widget-class structure for the class being initialized. The _Xwms_class_-part_initialize routine uses the additional class passed in to identify the widget class of the subpart being initialized. It then calls the class_part_initialize method of that subpart rather than the widget class that is being initialized.

Some methods pass return values back to their callers. An example of this type of method is set_values. The following example, using the xmText_set_values method, shows how these are handled:

```
Boolean xmText_set_values (old, request, new, args, num_args)
    Widget old;
    Widget request;
    Widget new;
    ArgList args;
    Cardinal *num_args;
{
    return (_Xwms_set_values (old, request, new, args, num_args,
        xmTextWidgetClass));
}
```

In summary, the purpose of initialization is to set up a linked list of data structures that contains one record for each widget class that can be monitored. Each of these records contains pointers to one-line methods that will be called instead of the class's original methods. These one-line methods are installed automatically by the WMS package after calls to XwmsSelectMethod are made. The method installation process is described in the following subsection.

METHOD SELECTION AND INSTALLATION

As described earlier, methods are selected for monitoring by calling the XwmsSelect-Method() routine. XwmsSelectMethod() is passed a widget class and method mask that together identify which method(s) should be monitored.

XwmsSelectMethod first checks to see if the WMS package is initialized. If it is not, Xwms-SelectMethod performs the initialization as previously described. Initializing the library in this manner eliminates an initialization call that an application programmer is otherwise forced to make.

After the package is initialized, the linked list of widget-class information created during initialization is searched for the widget class passed to XwmsSelectMethod(). If the record cannot be found, it indicates that the programmer is trying to monitor a widget that the package does not know about.

After retrieving the record from the linked list, a WMS extension to the Core part of the widget class is searched for. If the extension record cannot be found, it is created and linked to the extension field of the Core part of the widget-class record. If the extension is found, it indicates that XwmsSelectMethod() previously had been called to monitor other methods of this widget class.

At this point the WMS methods can be installed. Installing a method means saving the original widget-class method in the extension record and modifying the Core part of the widget class to contain the corresponding one-line method. Figure 1 shows the XmLabel widget-class structures before and after a call to XwmsSelectMethod to monitor the set_values method of the XmLabel widget class. If a method selected for monitoring is NULL, there are no statistics to collect, and no installation occurs.

The installation of methods that are inherited from a superclass must be deferred until after class part initialization for the widget class has been completed. Method inheritance is indicated by specifying a special constant, XtInheritExpose(), in a class record for a particular method. The class_part_initialize method of the widget class that defined the inheritance constant replaces it with the actual method to be inherited. Because class part initialization is chained in a superclass-to-subclass direction, we know that when the class_part_initialize method of a class is called, all inherited methods specified in its Core class part record will already have been replaced by the actual methods. Only at this point can WMS installation of these methods occur. Consequently, the WMS package defers installation of the realize, resize, expose, set_values_almost, accept_-focus, query_geometry, and display_accelerator methods until class_part_initialization. If the class_part_initialize method has not been explicitly selected for monitoring, or if a widget class has no class_part_ini-

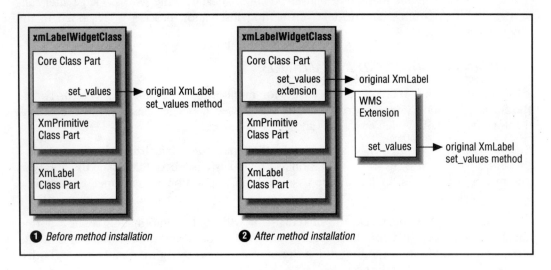

FIGURE 1: *The xmLabel Widget Class Before and After
WMS Installation of the set_values Method*

`tialize` method, the WMS package forces a special `class_part_initialize` method to be called to do this deferred installation.

METHOD EXECUTION

Methods can be executed by the Xt Intrinsics or by another method. In either case the behavior of the WMS package is the same. Figure 2 shows the calling sequence of the `set_values` method of a widget class that has been selected for monitoring.

Step 1 indicates that the `set_values` method of the class has been called. This method is the one-line `set_values` method linked to the class record during method installation. It calls the corresponding WMS method, `_Xwms_set_values` in this example, passing it the standard parameters and the widget class of the method that is being executed as an additional parameter.

The `_Xwms_set_values` method (step 2) uses the widget class passed to it to find the WMS extension record. It then displays trace output indicating that the method has been entered and, using the extension record, calls the original `expose` method for the widget class (step 3). After the original `expose` method completes and returns, `_XwmsStatEntry` is called to store the statistics in the WMS database (step 4).

MONITORING A CUSTOM WIDGET CLASS

In many cases, developers want to monitor custom widget classes. In fact, this may be where the WMS package is the most beneficial. The trace output provides valuable feedback

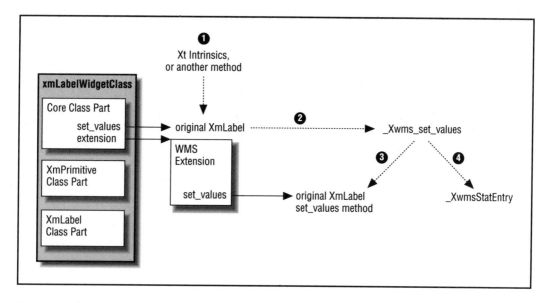

FIGURE 2: *The Calling Sequence of a Core Class Method is Shown by the Dotted Lines*

that identifies when the methods of the class are called. The statistical reports provide metrics that allow the widget-class developer to measure the performance of the widget as it is being developed, debugged, and optimized.

To monitor a custom widget class, the developer must first create a custom WMS method file that contains 15 one-line methods and a special initialization routine. Each of the one-line methods calls a corresponding internal WMS method. Each internal WMS method executes the widget class's original method and performs the method monitoring. Examples of these one-line methods were presented earlier in this paper, in the section "WMS Initialization." The special initialization routine is responsible for filling in the fields of a structure that is passed to it. The structure contains one field for the widget-class pointer and one field for each of the 15 Core class methods. Each of these fields is set to point to the corresponding one-line method for the widget class. The following example contains a portion of this routine for a hypothetical custom clock widget:

```
void _Xwms_init_Clock (coreMethods)
    CoreMethods coreMethods;
{
    /* initialize label fields */
    coreMethods->wc = ClockWidgetClass;
    coreMethods->class_initialize = xmClock_class_initialize;
    coreMethods->class_part_initialize =
        xmClock_class_part_initialize;
    coreMethods->initialize = xmClock_initialize;
```

```
coreMethods->initialize_hook = xmClock_initialize_hook;
coreMethods->realize = xmClock_realize;
   .
   .
   .

}
```

The custom WMS method file for the widget class must be linked with any application that wants to monitor methods of that class. To initiate monitoring of the custom widget-class methods, the application must first call the routine XwmsInstallWidgetClass, passing it the address of the initialization routine. XwmsInstallWidgetClass ensures that the custom widget class is a member of the set of widget classes that the WMS package knows about and can monitor.

To begin monitoring methods of the custom widget class, the developer calls XwmsSelect-Method the same way that it is called to monitor any other widget-class methods. Note that the custom widget class must be installed (by means of XwmsInstallWidgetClass) before methods can be selected for monitoring.

COMPONENTS OF THE WMS PACKAGE

The WMS package is composed of a library, four analysis utilities (described earlier), a database specification, and sample code. This section describes each of these components in more detail. The code is on *export.lcs.mit.edu* in the file *wms-1.0.tar.Z*.

THE XWMS LIBRARY

The five subroutines of the *Xwms* library can be grouped into three categories: method selection, output control, and widget-class installation.

Method selection

Two method-selection subroutines are provided to turn method tracing and statistics collection on and off for particular widget classes and methods. XwmsSelect-Method() is used to activate the monitoring of a widget class's methods. XwmsDeselectMethod() is used to turn off the monitoring of methods previously selected to be monitored.

Output contro

Two output-control subroutines are provided. XwmsTracing is used to toggle the trace capability on and off. The default behavior is for tracing to be on. This routine can be used to selectively turn tracing on or off during the execution of an application. It is useful when tracing only part of an application is desired. XwmsStatFile is used to specify the database filename. All statistics reported by the WMS package are written to this file. The default file name is *wms.data*.

Widget-class installation

One subroutine, `XwmsInstallWidgetClass()`, is provided so that custom widget classes can be monitored. This routine initializes data structures for the widget class needed by the WMS package and calls an initialization routine provided for the widget class. `XwmsInstallWidgetClass()` must be called before `XwmsSelectMethod()` for a custom widget class.

THE XWMS DATABASE

The *Xwms* database is the repository for statistical information captured by the WMS package. Each entry stored in this database has the following description and type:

- Method name: This is the name of the method that was called. Its type is `char32`.
- Method class: This is the widget class that the method belongs to. Its type is `char32`.
- Widget name: This is the name of the widget passed to the method. Its type is `char32`.
- Widget class: This is the name of the widget class of the widget passed to the method. Its type is `char32`.

These four fields correspond to those produced by the trace output. The following two additional fields represent the total time spent in the method. This includes any time spent in other methods that may have been called directly by this widget or indirectly due to a call to the Intrinsics (that is, `XtResizeWidget`).

- Seconds: This is the number of seconds spent in the method. It is usually 0, and its type is `long`.
- Nanoseconds: This is the number of nanoseconds spent in the method. Its type is `long`.

I hope that the preceding description of the database format will inspire users of the WMS package to write their own analysis applications.

XWMS SAMPLE CODE

Two distinct forms of sample code are provided: a widget-class template and sample programs. The widget-class template shows the code needed for monitoring a custom widget. Installation of the widget class is installed by calling the routine `XwmsInstallWidgetClass()`. The sample programs and their output are included to demonstrate the use of the WMS library routines.

USING THE WMS PACKAGE

To monitor the methods of a widget class only a few lines of code need to be added to an application. These additions are summarized in the following four steps. The sample programs in the appendices to this paper can be used for reference.

1. *Include the appropriate widget-class include files.* The public include file for any widget class that is to be monitored must be included. If an instance of the widget class is used by your program, this file may be already included. Because you can monitor the methods of any widget class, you may end up including a file for a widget class that you do not create any instances of and that would not otherwise be included.

2. *Include the WMS include file.* The file *wms.h* must be included. This file defines data structures and constants used by the WMS package.

3. *Specify the statistics file name.* This is an optional step used to change the name of the statistics file from the default value of *wms.data*. Call the routine XwmsStatFile, passing it the desired name of the statistics file. This call must be made before the first call to XwmsSelectMethod; otherwise it will have no effect.

4. *Select the widget classes and methods to monitor.* Use the routine XwmsSelect-Method to specify the methods of widget classes to be monitored. This can be done anywhere in a program. In the examples provided, and in most cases, it will be done at the beginning of the program.

To compile your program make sure that the compiler can find the *wms.h* include file. Linking your program requires including two WMS libraries in the link command. The first is the Core WMS library; the second one is for the widget set you are using. For example, to link a Motif-based program using the WMS package, use the following link command:

```
% cc -o <executable> <objects> $(LIBS)/wms.a $(LIBS)/motif.a -lXm -lXt -lX11
```

where $(LIBS) is the directory that contains the WMS libraries.

At this point the program can be executed, causing debugging output to be sent to the specified file.

FUTURE WORK

This section describes possible enhancements to be included in future versions of the WMS package.

The first major enhancement to the WMS package is support for tracing the methods of other Xt Intrinsics–supplied widget classes. The most interesting of these is the Composite widget class. Support will be added to trace and collect statistics on the four methods added by the Composite widget class—geometry_manager, change_managed, insert_-child, and delete_child. This will provide insight into geometry management and the geometry negotiating that goes on among manager widgets, their parents, and their children. It will also provide a way to quantify the performance differences that are realized when widgets are managed in different orders. Support may be added also for the Constraint class (the initialize, destroy, set_values, and get_values_hook methods) and for the Shell widget class (the root_geometry_manager method).

A second possible enhancement is to incorporate tracing callback routines. This capability would allow the programmer to specify a particular routine that would be called every time a method of a specified widget class is called. The programmer could then do custom tracing whenever the method was called. The callback routine would be passed the same arguments as the method and would have a return type of `void`.

A third possible enhancement involves extending the WMS data analysis tools to include graphical user interfaces (GUIs). A GUI for these tools would make it easier to view and use the data collected in the WMS database.

One final possible enhancement is to increase the breadth of metrics collected by the WMS package. The WMS package provides the hooks needed to collect statistics on any resource that the underlying operating system provides programmatic access to. The usefulness of this, however, is not yet clear to me.

SUMMARY

I believe that the tools presented in this paper can be useful to a wide range of audiences. Beginners who are seeking greater insight into the Xt Intrinsics and the implementation of widget classes can learn a great deal by monitoring the methods of different types of widgets. Application developers who are seeking to better understand the performance overhead imposed by widgets, and the ways their applications interact with widget methods, can generate reports that quantify the overhead of methods down to the level of a specific method for a specific widget instance. Finally, widget developers who are debugging and optimizing their code can generate reports that allow them to measure and compare the performances of different versions of the widget code.

Developing and also using the WMS package have been very educational for me. By monitoring the methods of widget classes in even the simplest programs, I have learned a great deal about how the Intrinsics works, how certain widget classes are implemented, and how the overhead is imposed by methods on an application. I have tried to share some of this information in the examples presented in this paper.

APPENDIX A

```
#include <Xm/Label.h>
#include <Xm/PushB.h>
#include <Xm/ToggleB.h>

#include "wms.h"

main (argc, argv)
int argc;
char *argv[];
{
    Widget toplevel, button;
    XtAppContext app;
```

```
    XmString xmlabel;

    XwmsStatFile ("test1.stats");
    XwmsSelectMethod (xmLabelWidgetClass, AllMethodsMask);
    XwmsSelectMethod (xmPushButtonWidgetClass, AllMethodsMask);
    XwmsSelectMethod (applicationShellWidgetClass, AllMethodsMask);

    toplevel = XtVaAppInitialize (&app, "Test1", NULL, 0,
        &argc, argv, NULL, NULL);

    xmlabel = XmStringCreateSimple ("Hello World");

    button = XtVaCreateManagedWidget ("button",
        xmPushButtonWidgetClass, toplevel,
        XmNlabelString, xmlabel,
        NULL);
    XmStringFree (xmlabel);

    XtRealizeWidget (toplevel);

    XtAppMainLoop (app);
}
```

APPENDIX B

```
#include <Xm/RowColumn.h>
#include <Xm/Label.h>
#include <Xm/PushB.h>

#include "wms.h"

static int counter = 0;
static int interval = 1;

main (argc, argv)
int argc;
char *argv[];
{
    Widget toplevel, rc, inc, dec, label, interval;
    XmString xmstr;
    XtAppContext app;
    void increment ();
    void decrement ();
    void set_interval ();
```

```
        XwmsStatFile ("test2.stats");
        XwmsSelectMethod (xmLabelWidgetClass, AllMethodsMask);
        XwmsSelectMethod (xmPushButtonWidgetClass, AllMethodsMask);
        XwmsSelectMethod (xmRowColumnWidgetClass, AllMethodsMask);
        XwmsSelectMethod (applicationShellWidgetClass, AllMethodsMask);

        toplevel = XtVaAppInitialize (&app, "Test2", NULL, 0,
            &argc, argv, NULL, NULL);

        rc = XtVaCreateManagedWidget ("rc",
            xmRowColumnWidgetClass, toplevel,
            NULL);

        label = XtVaCreateManagedWidget ("0",
            xmLabelWidgetClass, rc,
            NULL);

        inc = XtVaCreateManagedWidget ("Increment",
            xmPushButtonWidgetClass, rc,
            NULL);
        XtAddCallback (inc, XmNactivateCallback, increment, label);

        dec = XtVaCreateManagedWidget ("Decrement",
            xmPushButtonWidgetClass, rc,
            NULL);
        XtAddCallback (dec, XmNactivateCallback, decrement, label);

        xmstr = XmStringCreateSimple ("Increment by 1");
        interval = XtVaCreateManagedWidget ("Interval",
            xmPushButtonWidgetClass, rc,
            XmNlabelString, xmstr,
            NULL);
        XmStringFree (xmstr);
        XtAddCallback (interval, XmNactivateCallback, set_interval, NULL);

        XtRealizeWidget (toplevel);

        XtAppMainLoop (app);
}

void increment (w, label, cbs)
    Widget w;
    Widget label;
```

```
    XmPushButtonCallbackStruct *cbs;
{
    XmString str;
    char cstr[25];

    counter += interval;
    sprintf (cstr, "%d", counter);
    str = XmStringCreateSimple (cstr);
    XtVaSetValues (label,
        XmNlabelString, str,
        NULL);
    XmStringFree (str);
}

void decrement (w, label, cbs)
    Widget w;
    Widget label;
    XmPushButtonCallbackStruct *cbs;
{
    XmString str;
    char cstr[25];

    counter -= interval;
    sprintf (cstr, "%d", counter);
    str = XmStringCreateSimple (cstr);
    XtVaSetValues (label,
        XmNlabelString, str,
        NULL);
    XmStringFree (str);
}

void set_interval (w, cd, cbs)
    Widget w;
    XtPointer cd;
    XmPushButtonCallbackStruct *cbs;
{
    XmString str;
    char cstr[25];

    interval *= 2;
    sprintf (cstr, "Increment by %d", interval);
    str = XmStringCreateSimple (cstr);
    XtVaSetValues (w,
```

```
        XmNlabelString, str,
        NULL);
    XmStringFree (str);
}
```

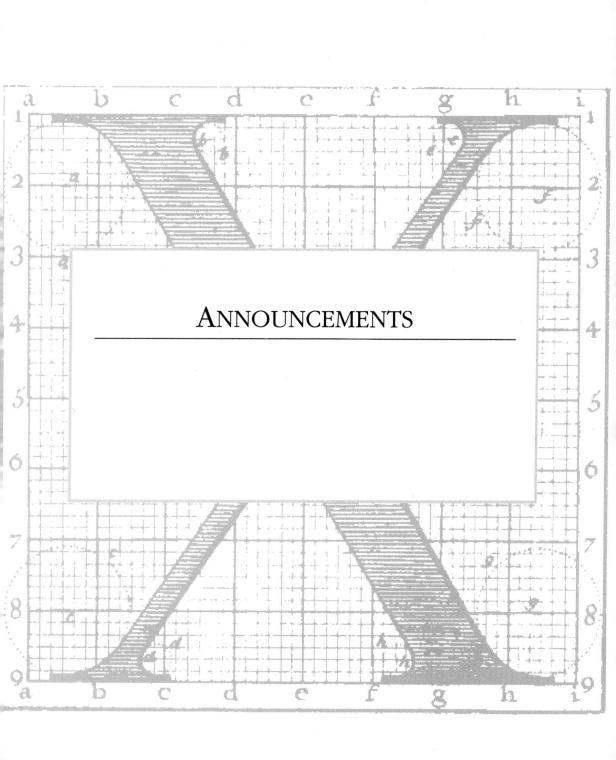

ANNOUNCEMENTS

X Professional Organization Membership Application Form

The *X Professional Organization* is a user oriented organization providing both goods and services to the users of The X Window System. Members receive the XPO newsletter quarterly, a subscription to *The X Resource* (a quarterly publication by O'Reilly & Associates), and discounts on books and other X related products.

Membership Pricing:

1 year membership, U.S. funds

	Associate	Regular	Special
USA	$35.00	$100.00	$120.00
Canada/Mexico	$40.00	$105.00	$135.00
Europe/Africa	$45.00	$125.00	$175.00
Asia/Australia	$50.00	$130.00	$185.00

Complete this form and mail with payment to:

X Professional Organization
P.O. Box 78
Beltsville, MD 20704 USA
Fax: (410) 799-7197

Membership Category:

Associate	Quarterly Newsletter
Regular	Quarterly Newsletter + *The X Resource*
Special	Quarterly Newsletter + *The X Resource* + X Resource Special Supplements

Please provide the following information:

Associate ☐   Regular ☐   Special ☐

Name —————————————————————————
Company —————————————————————————
Address —————————————————————————
City/State/Zip —————————————————————————
Country —————————————————————————
Telephone —————————————————————————

email —————————————————————————

XPO will process purchase orders. Please provide this order form and note "bill to" and "ship to" addresses with your purchase order.

If you would like more information, email us at wbarker@wam.umd.edu or call (410) 799-7197

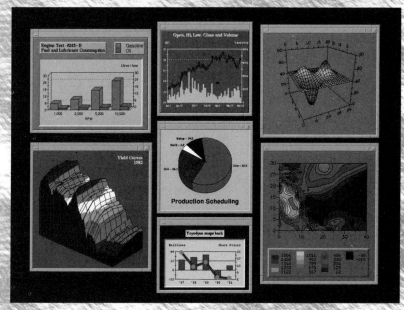

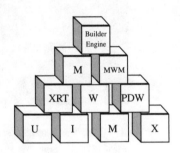

GUI BUILDING IS CHILD'S PLAY WITH XFACEMAKER

XFaceMaker's simple, intuitive layout, resource editors, and convenient dialog boxes make it easy to *create sophisticated interfaces using the Motif building blocks.* Version 2.0 of XFaceMaker is the only GUI builder that lets you create *new widget classes interactively.* And with templates, you can use object-oriented design and enforce style guidelines.

In XFaceMaker, you program the callbacks that specify interface behavior using our easy-to-use, C-like FACE scripting language. The built in FACE interpreter allows you to test the interface on the fly. Using FACE helps free you from the intricacies of Motif programming, saving you time without sacrificing performance or functionality.

99 Bedford Street
Boston, MA 02111
Tel: (617) 482-6393
Fax: (617) 482-9707
email info@nsl.com

57-59, Rue Lhomond
75005 Paris, FRANCE
Tél: (33) (1) 43 36 77 50
Fax: (1) 43 36 59 78

NON STANDARD LOGICS

THE Low DOWN
on High Performance Computing

High Performance Computing

By Kevin Dowd, 1st Edition June 1993
350 pages (est.), ISBN 1-56592-032-5, $25.95

This book is a "must" for anyone who needs to worry about computer performance, either as a software developer or as a buyer. But it also provides valuable insights for those among us who do relatively little programming and run mostly third-party application software. Even if you never touch a line of code, *High Performance Computing* will give you a feel for how the most recent generation of computer hardware works.

If you work with computers, you owe it to yourself to understand the new directions that workstation architecture has taken in the last half decade, including RISC-based workstation architectures like DEC Alpha/AXP, the IBM RS/6000 and the HP 9000/700 series.

This book covers everything, from the basics of modern workstation architecture, to structuring benchmarks, to squeezing more performance out of critical applications. It also explains how optimizing compilers work: it discusses

what a good compiler can do for you and, more important, what a good compiler can't do—and what you have to do yourself.

The author also discusses techniques for improving memory access patterns and taking advantage of parallelism. The book closes with a look at the high-performance future: parallel computers, including exotic distributed memory multiprocessors, and the more "garden-variety" shared memory processors that are already appearing on people's desktops. *High Performance Computing* pays special attention to memory issues; perhaps the most important story in high performance computing (and one seldom told by vendors) is the increasing disparity between CPU speeds and memory speeds.

Another valuable section of the book discusses the benchmarking process: how to evaluate a computer's performance. Kevin Dowd discusses several of the "standard" industry benchmarks, explaining what they measure and what they don't. He also explains how to set up your own benchmark: how to structure the code, how to measure the results, and how to interpret them.

BACK ISSUES OF THE X RESOURCE

Back issues are available to North American customers directly from the publisher for $22.50 each plus shipping (see inside front cover). Overseas customers should contact our Overseas Distributors (listed two pages hence). The journal is also carried by many U.S. and foreign bookstores.

ISSUE 0: FALL 1991

BACK ISSUES OF THE X RESOURCE

ISSUE 1: WINTER 1992

PROCEEDINGS
6TH ANNUAL X TECHNICAL CONFERENCE
SPONSORED BY THE X CONSORTIUM
JANUARY 13-15, 1992

BACK ISSUES OF THE X RESOURCE

ISSUE 2: SPRING 1992

BACK ISSUES OF THE X RESOURCE

ISSUE 3: SUMMER 1992

BACK ISSUES OF THE X RESOURCE

ISSUE 4: FALL 1992

BACK ISSUES OF THE X RESOURCE

ISSUE 5: WINTER 1993

BACK ISSUES OF THE X RESOURCE

ISSUE 6: SPRING 1993

The best source of timely, in-depth articles on the X Window System today! Subscribe now and save 28% off the single issue price.

❏ **$65 Quarterly Issues**

❏ **$90 Quarterly Issues** plus Special Issues: public review specifications for proposed X Consortium standards and introductory explanations of the issues involved.

Extra shipping for foreign orders: Canada/Mexico $5/$10 (with special Issues), Europe/Africa $25/50; Asia/Australia $30/$60. Foreign orders must be by credit card or in US dollars drawn from a US bank.

Name _____ Company _____

Address _____ City/State/Zip _____

Country _____ e-mail _____

Bill to my Credit Card or call (800) 998-9938 (US and Canada)   XRI5

❏ Visa   ❏ Mastercard   ❏ American Express

Account Number _____ Exp. Date _____

Name as it appears on card _____ Signature _____

The best source of timely, in-depth articles on the X Window System today! Subscribe now and save 28% off the single issue price.

❏ **$65 Quarterly Issues**

❏ **$90 Quarterly Issues** plus Special Issues: public review specifications for proposed X Consortium standards and introductory explanations of the issues involved.

Extra shipping for foreign orders: Canada/Mexico $5/$10 (with special Issues), Europe/Africa $25/50; Asia/Australia $30/$60. Foreign orders must be by credit card or in US dollars drawn from a US bank.

Name _____ Company _____

Address _____ City/State/Zip _____

Country _____ e-mail _____

Bill to my Credit Card or call (800) 998-9938 (US and Canada)   XRI5

❏ Visa   ❏ Mastercard   ❏ American Express

Account Number _____ Exp. Date _____

Name as it appears on card _____ Signature _____

NAME_____

COMPANY_____

ADDRESS_____

CITY _____ STATE _____ ZIP _____

BUSINESS REPLY MAIL

FIRST CLASS MAIL PERMIT NO. 80 SEBASTOPOL, CA

POSTAGE WILL BE PAID BY ADDRESSEE

O'REILLY & ASSOCIATES, INC.

103 Morris Street Suite A
Sebastopol CA 95472-9902

NAME_____

COMPANY_____

ADDRESS_____

CITY _____ STATE _____ ZIP _____

BUSINESS REPLY MAIL

FIRST CLASS MAIL PERMIT NO. 80 SEBASTOPOL, CA

POSTAGE WILL BE PAID BY ADDRESSEE

O'REILLY & ASSOCIATES, INC.

103 Morris Street Suite A
Sebastopol CA 95472-9902